LPI
Security
Essentials
Study Guide

LPI
Security
Essentials
Study Guide
Exam 020-100

David Clinton

A Wiley Brand

Acknowledgments

I would like to thank my wife for all her help and support through the long and demanding process of writing this book. And, once again, I'm indebted to all the great people at Wiley who helped me turn a plain old manuscript into a great teaching tool.

About the Author

David Clinton is a Linux server admin who has worked with IT infrastructure in both academic and enterprise environments. He has authored and co-authored technology books—including *AWS Certified Solutions Architect Study Guide: Associate SAA-C03 Exam, Fourth Edition* (Sybex, 2022)—and created dozens of video courses teaching Amazon Web Services and Linux administration, server virtualization, and IT security.

In a previous life, David spent 20 years as a high school teacher. He currently lives in Toronto, Canada, with his wife and family and can be reached through his website: `https://bootstrap-it.com`.

Contents at a Glance

Introduction   *xiii*

Assessment Test   *xvii*

Chapter 1   Using Digital Resources Responsibly   1

Chapter 2   What Are Vulnerabilities and Threats?   17

Chapter 3   Controlling Access to Your Assets   37

Chapter 4   Controlling Network Connections   63

Chapter 5   Encrypting Your Data at Rest   85

Chapter 6   Encrypting Your Moving Data   97

Chapter 7   Risk Assessment   113

Chapter 8   Configuring System Backups and Monitoring   127

Chapter 9   Resource Isolation Design Patterns   143

Appendix   Answers to Review Questions   155

        Index   *167*

Contents

Introduction   *xiii*

Assessment Test   *xvii*

Chapter   1   Using Digital Resources Responsibly   1

Protecting Personal Rights   3
Protecting Digital Privacy   5
What Is Personal Data?   5
Where Might My Personal Data Be Hanging Out?   5
What Are My Responsibilities as a Site Administrator?   7
Can Escaped Genies Be Forced Back into Their Bottles?   8
What Can I Do as a User?   8
Establishing Authenticity   9
Think About the Source   9
Be Aware of Common Threat Categories   10
Summary   11
Exam Essentials   11
Review Questions   13

Chapter   2   What Are Vulnerabilities and Threats?   17

The Basics: What Are We Trying to Accomplish Here?   19
What Are Vulnerabilities and Threats?   19
What Can Be Exploited?   20
Who's Doing the Exploiting?   21
Why Do They Attack?   22
Common Vulnerabilities   23
Software Vulnerabilities   23
Hardware Vulnerabilities   24
Bioware Vulnerabilities   25
Digital Espionage   25
USB Devices   25
Backdoors   26
Wireless Entry Points   26
Stolen Credentials   27
Data Breaches   27
Identity Theft (Besides Breaches)   28
Malware   28
Network-Based Attacks   30
Man-in-the-Middle Attacks   30
Denial-of-Service and Distributed Denial-of-Service Attacks   30
Network Routing Attacks   30

		Cloud Computing and Digital Security	31
		Summary	31
		Exam Essentials	32
		Review Questions	33
Chapter	**3**	**Controlling Access to Your Assets**	**37**
		Controlling Physical Access	39
		Understanding Your Devices	39
		Protecting Your Devices	41
		Managing Authentication Through Effective Password Use	43
		Managing Authorization Through Permissions	49
		Controlling Network Access	50
		Firewalls	50
		Virus and Malware Protection	52
		Educating Your Users	54
		Controlling Software Sources	55
		PC Software Repositories	56
		Mobile Package Management	56
		Summary	57
		Exam Essentials	57
		Review Questions	59
Chapter	**4**	**Controlling Network Connections**	**63**
		Understanding Network Architecture	64
		The Transmission Control Protocol	64
		The Internet Protocol	65
		Understanding the Domain Name System	68
		Auditing Networks	69
		Network Auditing Tools	70
		Automating Audits	75
		Securing Networks	75
		Patch Your Software	76
		Physically Secure Your Infrastructure	76
		Secure Your Network Behavior	77
		Securing Your Wireless Connections	77
		Other Stuff	78
		Summary	78
		Exam Essentials	79
		Review Questions	80
Chapter	**5**	**Encrypting Your Data at Rest**	**85**
		What Is Encryption?	86
		Encryption Usage Patterns	89
		What Should You Encrypt?	89

Understanding Hashing vs. Encryption	90
What Are Blockchains?	91
Encryption Technologies	92
Summary	93
Exam Essentials	94
Review Questions	95

Chapter 6	**Encrypting Your Moving Data**	**97**
	Website Encryption	99
	Why You Should Use Encryption	100
	How Website Encryption Works	100
	Generating Certificates	103
	Email Encryption	104
	GNU Privacy Guard	105
	Does Gmail Encrypt Your Emails?	105
	Working with VPN Connections and Software Repositories	106
	Securing Your Actions Using VPNs	106
	Securing Transfers from Software Repositories	107
	Summary	108
	Exam Essentials	108
	Review Questions	109

Chapter 7	**Risk Assessment**	**113**
	Conducting Open-Source Intelligence Gathering	115
	Accessing Public Vulnerability Databases	116
	Vulnerability Data Frameworks	116
	Vulnerability Data Formats	117
	Vulnerability Data Metrics	118
	Vulnerability Data Management Tools	118
	Conducting Vulnerability Scans	119
	Conducting Penetration Tests	120
	Attack Vectors	121
	Tooling Frameworks	122
	Follow-Up	122
	Summary	122
	Exam Essentials	123
	Review Questions	124

Chapter 8	**Configuring System Backups and Monitoring**	**127**
	Why You Need to Get Backups Right the First Time	129
	Appreciating the Risks	130
	Spreading Your Backups Across Multiple Sites	131
	Testing Your Backups	132
	Meeting Regulatory Compliance	132

	Backup Types	133
	Incremental Backups	133
	Differential Backups	133
	Backup Life Cycles	134
	Multitier Backups	134
	Multisite Storage Solutions	134
	Disaster Recovery Planning	135
	Configuring Monitoring and Alerts	135
	Working with System Logs	136
	Intrusion Detection	137
	Summary	137
	Exam Essentials	138
	Review Questions	139
Chapter 9	**Resource Isolation Design Patterns**	**143**
	Configuring Network Firewalling	145
	Balancing Public and Private Networks	145
	Building Isolated Development Environments	146
	Working with Sandbox Environments	147
	Use Cases for Sandboxes	148
	Sandbox Designs	148
	Controlling Local System Access	150
	Configuring Mandatory Access Controls	150
	Setting Usage Quotas	151
	Summary	152
	Exam Essentials	152
	Review Questions	153
Appendix	**Answers to Review Questions**	**155**
	Chapter 1: Using Digital Resources Responsibly	156
	Chapter 2: What Are Vulnerabilities and Threats?	157
	Chapter 3: Controlling Access to Your Assets	158
	Chapter 4: Controlling Network Connections	160
	Chapter 5: Encrypting Your Data at Rest	161
	Chapter 6: Encrypting Your Moving Data	162
	Chapter 7: Risk Assessment	163
	Chapter 8: Configuring System Backups and Monitoring	165
	Chapter 9: Resource Isolation Design Patterns	166
	Index	*167*

Introduction

I often say that you earn the real payoff from a well-designed certification exam by carefully working through its objectives. Sure, having a pretty certificate to hang on your wall is nice. But the skills and understanding you'll gain from hitting all the key points of a program like this Security Essentials cert will take you a whole lot further.

The moment we connect our phones, laptops, and servers to the Internet, we're all living in a very dangerous neighborhood. And there's no single "set-it-and-forget-it" solution that'll reliably keep all the looming threats away. The only way you can even hope to protect yourself and your digital resources is to understand the kinds of vulnerabilities that could affect your infrastructure and the ways smart administration can maximize both harm prevention and mitigation. But there's more. Since the IT threat landscape changes so often, you'll also need to learn how to continuously monitor your infrastructure and keep up with developments in the technology world.

Whether you're a team manager, an IT professional, a developer, a data engineer, or even just a regular technology consumer, you'll be both safer and more effective at everything you do if you can understand and apply security best practices. So I encourage you to plan to take and pass the Linux Professional Institute's Security Essentials exam. But whatever your certification goals, you should definitely plan to master the content represented by the objectives. And this book was written to get you there.

Like the certification itself, the content in this *LPI Security Essentials Study Guide* is platform neutral. That means you can ignore the *Linux* in the title. Sure, the institute's initial mandate was to enable the broader adoption of the Linux operating system—and they've done a great job at it. But the same smart and highly experienced people who drive the institute's Linux curriculum development are also outstanding security professionals. And their expertise extends to all operating systems and all platform categories. If your equipment speaks binary, it's covered here.

Each of the book's chapters includes review questions to thoroughly test your understanding of the services you've seen. The questions were designed to help you realistically gauge your understanding and readiness for the exam. Although the difficulty level will vary between questions, it's all on target and relevant to both the exam and the real digital world. Once you complete a chapter's assessment, refer to Appendix A for the correct answers and detailed explanations.

What Does This Book Cover?

This book covers topics you need to know to prepare for the Security Essentials certification exam:

Chapter 1: Using Digital Resources Responsibly In this chapter you'll learn about protecting the digital rights and privacy of people with whom you interact,—including your own employees and the users of your services.

Chapter 2: What Are Vulnerabilities and Threats?   Here you'll discover the scope of the many classes of threats against your infrastructure, including digital espionage, stolen credentials, and malware.

Chapter 3: Controlling Access to Your Assets   Your first line of defense against the bad guys is the outer edge of your property. So learning to manage physical and network access to your resources is a big deal.

Chapter 4: Controlling Network Connections   Before you can effectively audit and secure your networks, you'll need to understand how IP/TCP networking actually works. This chapter will introduce you to both general networking administration and the basics of network security.

Chapter 5: Encrypting Your Data at Rest   What can I say? Obscuring your important data stores from prying eyes is a critical component of security. Learn why, how, and where it should be done.

Chapter 6: Encrypting Your Moving Data   In this chapter you'll learn about website and email encryption, along with the care and feeding of virtual private networks (VPNs).

Chapter 7: Risk Assessment   You'll never know how secure your infrastructure is until it comes under attack. Now who would you prefer launches this first attack? This is something you'd rather want to do yourself through the services of vulnerability scanners and penetration testers.

Chapter 8: Configuring System Backups and Monitoring   Despite all your best efforts, you're going to lose important data at some point. If you're properly backed up, then you're singing. And the sooner you find out there's bad stuff happening, the happier your song will be.

Chapter 9: Resource Isolation Design Patterns   The final chapter will discuss some important security design tools, like firewalls, sandboxes, and OS access control software.

About the Exam

Here's the Linux Professional Institute's description of the certification's "minimally qualified candidate":

> "The candidate has a basic understanding of common security threats of using computers, networks, connected devices, and IT services on premises and in the cloud. The candidate understands common ways to prevent and mitigate attacks against their personal devices and data. Furthermore, the candidate is able to use encryption to secure data transferred through a network and stored on storage devices and in the cloud. The candidate is able to apply common security best practices, protect private information,

and secure their identity. The candidate is able to securely use IT services and to take responsibility for securing their personal computing devices, applications, accounts, and online profiles."

Exam Objectives

1 021 Security Concepts

    1.1 021.1 Goals, Roles and Actors (weight: 1)

    1.2 021.2 Risk Assessment and Management (weight: 2)

    1.3 021.3 Ethical Behavior (weight: 2)

2 022 Encryption

    2.1 022.1 Cryptography and Public Key Infrastructure (weight: 3)

    2.2 022.2 Web Encryption (weight: 2)

    2.3 022.3 Email Encryption (weight: 2)

    2.4 022.4 Data Storage Encryption (weight: 2)

3 023 Node, Device and Storage Security

    3.1 023.1 Hardware Security (weight: 2)

    3.2 023.2 Application Security (weight: 2)

    3.3 023.3 Malware (weight: 3)

    3.4 023.4 Data Availability (weight: 2)

4 024 Network and Service Security

    4.1 024.1 Networks, Network Services and the Internet (weight: 4)

    4.2 024.2 Network and Internet Security (weight: 3)

    4.3 024.3 Network Encryption and Anonymity (weight: 3)

5 025 Identity and Privacy

    5.1 025.1 Identity and Authentication (weight: 3)

    5.2 025.2 Information Confidentiality and Secure Communication (weight: 2)

    5.3 025.3 Privacy Protection (weight: 2)

Objective Map

The exam covers five larger domains, with each domain broken down into objectives. The following table lists each domain and its weighting in the exam, along with the chapters in the book where that domain's objectives are primarily covered.

Objective	Weight	Chapter(s)
1. Security Concepts		
1.1 Goals, Roles and Actors	1	1, 2
1.2 Risk Assessment and Management	2	4, 7, 9
1.3 Ethical Behavior	2	1, 7
2. Encryption		
2.1 Cryptography and Public Key Infrastructure	3	5, 6
2.2 Web Encryption	2	6
2.3 Email Encryption	2	6
2.4 Data Storage Encryption	2	5
3. Node, Device and Storage Security		
3.1 Hardware Security	2	2, 3
3.2 Application Security	2	3, 6
3.3 Malware	3	2, 3
3.4 Data Availability	2	8
4. Network and Service Security		
4.1 Networks, Network Services and the Internet	4	2, 4, 9
4.2 Network and Internet Security	3	2, 4
4.3 Network Encryption and Anonymity	3	1, 2, 6
5. Identity and Privacy		
5.1 Identity and Authentication	3	3, 6
5.2 Information Confidentiality and Secure Communication	2	1, 2
5.3 Privacy Protection	2	1

How to Contact the Publisher

If you believe you have found a mistake in this book, please bring it to our attention. At John Wiley & Sons, we understand how important it is to provide our customers with accurate content, but even with our best efforts an error may occur.

To submit your possible errata, please email it to our Customer Service Team at wileysupport@wiley.com with the subject line "Possible Book Errata Submission."

Assessment Test

1. Which of the following digital tools is the most likely to collect—and possibly share—your private information without your knowledge?
   A. A programming integrated development environment (IDE)
   B. A USB device
   C. A web browser
   D. A command-line interface (CLI) environment

2. What is a backdoor?
   A. A network port opened to permit remote SSH access
   B. An undocumented access route to a computer system
   C. A software package management system that runs in the background
   D. The rear plate on a rack-mounted server

3. Which of these device types share information wirelessly without the need for authentication?
   A. RFID
   B. Wi-Fi
   C. Cellular networks
   D. Ethernet

4. Which of the following are components that are often protected by passwords? (Choose three.)
   A. Connecting to the Internet
   B. UEFI firmware
   C. Screen saver
   D. OS logon

5. Which of the following software tools can analyze network packets?
   A. Nmap
   B. SSH
   C. Wireshark
   D. TCP/IP

6. Which of the following is a common drawback associated with the use of asymmetric encryption?
   A. It's a new and relatively untested technology.
   B. It takes a relatively long time to process transactions.
   C. It requires the potentially risky transfer of a decryption key.
   D. It requires significant compute resources to manage.

7. What makes strong website encryption so important?

    A. It's the best way to protect the data on your storage drives.

    B. It's a critical tool for reducing system memory usage.

    C. It's the best way to ensure that your website data reaches your clients intact and without being intercepted.

    D. It's the primary defense against DNS poisoning.

8. What best describes the purpose of vulnerability scanning?

    A. To test your infrastructure's defenses

    B. To search for system or network misconfigurations

    C. To discover and implement mitigation operations

    D. To simulate an actual attack against your infrastructure

9. What process provides ongoing monitoring of your system that can alert admins when dangerous events occur?

    A. Intrusion detection

    B. Penetration testing

    C. Efficiency audits

    D. Unit testing

10. What type of service can most effectively filter packets coming into and out of a network?

    A. Block device managers

    B. Network firewalls

    C. Application load balancers

    D. Auto scalers

Answers to Assessment Test

1. C. IDEs and CLIs are not, by default, configured to connect to remote services—much less share data with them. The vast majority of USB devices don't contain self-launching scripts that are capable of manipulating data.

2. B. A backdoor is an unauthorized and undocumented way to access a computer operating system—usually left open with the goal of illegally gaining control of local data and system activities.

3. A. Wi-Fi has built-in authentication methods, and cell networks require validation (through a SIM card, for instance). Ethernet connections are not wireless.

4. B, C, D. It's not common—or even necessarily easy—to prevent passwordless access to application software (like a web browser). Screen savers, BIOS and UEFI interfaces, and OS logins all have built-in password protection (if enabled).

5. C. Nmap can identify vulnerable or hostile network devices, but it doesn't analyze packets. SSH is a tool for launching a secure remote session. TCP/IP is a set of network communication protocols.

6. D. Asymmetric encryption is not a new technology. It's unlikely that you would notice any delays in processing. There's no need to transfer private keys for asymmetric encryption.

7. C. Website encryption won't protect your local data and won't reduce memory usage. While it can help prevent DNS poisoning, it's not the primary defense.

8. B. Testing defenses or simulating attacks is closer to "penetration testing." I have no idea what "discovering and implementing mitigation operations" might mean.

9. A. Penetration testing and efficiency audits don't provide ongoing monitoring, and unit tests are for DevOps teams, not sysadmins.

10. B. Load balancers are primarily concerned with directing traffic rather than filtering it. Auto scalers are built to adjust resource availability. Block device managers deal with storage volumes, not network traffic.

Chapter

1

Using Digital Resources Responsibly

THE LPI SECURITY ESSENTIALS EXAM TOPICS COVERED IN THIS CHAPTER INCLUDE THE FOLLOWING:

- ✓ **021.1 Goals, roles and actors**
  - Understanding of the importance of IT security

- ✓ **021.3 Ethical behavior**
  - Understanding the implications for others of actions taken related to security
  - Handling information about security vulnerabilities responsibly
  - Handling confidential information responsibly
  - Awareness of personal, financial, ecological, and social implication of errors and outages in information technology services

- ✓ **024.3 Network encryption and anonymity**
  - Understanding of the concepts of TOR
  - Awareness of the Darknet

- ✓ **025.2 Information confidentiality and secure communication (weight: 2)**
  - Understanding the implications and risks of data leaks and intercepted communication
  - Understanding of phishing and social engineering and scamming
  - Understanding the concepts of email spam filters

✓ **025.3 Privacy protection**

- Understanding of the importance of personal information

- Understanding of how personal information can be used for a malicious purpose

- Understanding of the concepts of information gathering, profiling, and user tracking

- Managing profile privacy settings on social media platforms and online services

- Understanding of the risk of publishing personal information

- Understanding of the rights regarding personal information (e.g., GDPR)

"With great power comes great responsibility."

Words of wisdom. That's the message displayed for administrators when they log in for the first time to many Linux distributions. Who said those words first? Aristotle? Kant? Nope. Spiderman's uncle. But hey, accept the truth from any source.

While we'll discuss protecting yourself from attack at length later in the book, this chapter is all about responsibilities. It's about your responsibilities both as a *consumer* of computer technologies and as an *administrator* of computer technologies. It's your job to make sure nothing you do online or with your devices causes harm to anyone's assets.

How is all this relevant to the world of information technology (IT) and, specifically, to IT security? Computers amplify your strengths. No matter how much you can remember, how fast you can calculate, or how many people's lives you can touch, it'll never come close to the scope of what you can do with a computing device and a network. So, given the power inherent in digital technologies and the depth of chaos such power can unleash, you *need* to understand how it can all go wrong before you set off to use it for good.

The rest of this chapter will explore the importance of considering how your actions can impact people's personal and property rights and privacy and how you can both ensure and assess the authenticity of online information.

I'm not a lawyer, and this book doesn't pretend to offer legal advice, so we're not going to discuss some of the more esoteric places where individual rights can come into conflict with events driven by technology. Instead, we'll keep it simple. People should be able to go about their business and enjoy their interactions with each other without having to worry about having physical, financial, or emotional injury imposed on them. And you should be ready to do whatever is necessary to avoid or prevent such injuries.

Protecting Personal Rights

These days, the greatest technology-based threats to an individual's personal well-being will probably exist on one or another social media platform. Facebook, Twitter, LinkedIn, and other online sites present opportunities for anyone to reach out to and communicate with millions or even billions of other users. This can make it possible to build entire businesses or social advocacy movements in ways that would have been unthinkable just a few years back. But, as we all now know, it also makes it possible to spread dangerous scams, political mischief, and social conflict.

As the man said, "With great power comes great responsibility." Therefore, you need to be conscious of the possible impact of any interaction you undertake. This will be true not only for your use of your own social media or email/messaging accounts but also for any interactions taking place on sites or platforms you administrate. You could, for instance, be held legally responsible for anonymous comments left on your blog or for the use of email accounts belonging to your organization. It can be a hard balance to achieve. Are your policies unnecessarily allowing damaging content to be published or, alternatively, unfairly restricting innocuous content?

A helpful tool for maintaining perspective in these areas is to apply the *grandmother test*. What's that? Before posting a message or comment on any online forum, take a minute to read it over one or two more times and then ask yourself, "Would both my grandmothers approve of what I've written? Is there anything that would make them uncomfortable?" In other words, ask yourself whether anyone could reasonably feel threatened or bullied by what you're about to publish. The bottom line is to make generous use of common sense and goodwill.

With typical attention to such details, the social media community has come up with new names to describe each of the nastiest online threats. You should, unfortunately, be familiar with each of them.

Cyberstalking   Stalking isn't specific to online activities, but that doesn't make it any less frightening. In general terms, a stalker persistently follows and observes a target, often with the goal of forcing an unwanted reaction. In the online world, *cyberstalking* can include electronic monitoring of a target's online accounts and activities. Harassing cyberstalking can escalate beyond mere monitoring to include threats, slander, and identity theft.

Cybermobbing   Mobbing involves large groups of people banding together to engage in bullying behavior. The nature of many social networking platforms—in particular the prevalence of anonymous accounts and the ease by which users can connect to each other—lends itself to mob formation. Often, all it can take is a single public post expressing an unpopular position, and the power of tens of thousands of users can be brought to bear with the goal of making life miserable for the post's author.

Doxxing   Whether you present yourself to the online world using your real name or through an anonymous identity, you certainly don't want your complete personal profile to become public. Considering all the data that's already available on the Internet, it's often not hard for people with time on their hands to track down your physical address and private phone numbers. But making such information easily available on popular social media sites with the intention of causing the target harm is wrong—and, in some jurisdictions, also a crime. Victims of public doxxing have experienced relatively mild annoyances like middle-of-the-night pizza deliveries. But the practice has also proven deadly: it's been used as part of "swatting" attacks, where people call a victim's local police department claiming there's a violent crime in progress at the victim's address. More than one doxxer has been imprisoned for what, at the time, must have seemed like a clever prank.

Protecting Digital Privacy

Your primary concern must always be to secure the data under your control. But have you ever wondered why that is? What's the worst that could happen if copies of your data are stolen—after all, you'll still have the originals, right? Well, if your organization is in the business of profiting from innovations and complex, hard-to-reproduce technology stacks, then the consequences of data theft are obvious. But even if your data contains nothing more than private and personal information, there's a lot that can go wrong.

Let's explore all that by way of posing a few questions.

What Is Personal Data?

Your personal data is any information that relates to your health, employment, banking activities, close relationships, and interactions with government agencies. In most cases, you should have the legal right to expect that such information remains inaccessible to anyone without your permission.

But "personal data" could also be anything that you contributed with the reasonable expectation that it would remain private. That could include exchanges of emails and messages or recordings and transcripts of phone conversations. It should also include data—like your browser search history—saved to the storage devices used by your compute devices.

Businesses and government departments that handle many kinds of data must apply information classification systems to ensure that their data isn't mishandled. They might, therefore, label all data objects using designations like *confidential, classified,* and *restricted*. Clear policies based on those classifications should be enforced for the management of all that data.

Among other measures, organizations can seek to control the way their data is shared by imposing nondisclosure agreements (NDAs). Outside consultants doing work with such an organization might be required to sign an NDA that precisely defines limits for how the information they'll be shown should be handled.

You have the right to expect that social media platforms and other third-party organizations respect the privacy settings you choose for your accounts. However, it's your responsibility to ensure that your settings properly reflect your needs and preferences. You should make it a practice, from time to time, to revisit your account settings and, if necessary, update them.

Governments, citing national interest concerns, will reserve the right for their security and enforcement agencies to forcibly access your personal data where legally required. Of course, different governments will set the circumstances defining "legally required" according to their own standards. When you disagree, some jurisdictions permit legal appeal.

Where Might My Personal Data Be Hanging Out?

The short answer to that question is "probably lots of places you wouldn't approve." The long answer will begin with something like "I can tell you, but expect to become and remain deeply stressed and anxious." In other words, it won't be pretty. But since you asked, the following are some things to consider.

Browsing Histories

The digital history of the sites you've visited on your browser can take more than one form. Your browser can maintain its own log of the URLs of all the pages you've opened. Your browser's cache will hold some of the actual page elements (like graphic images) and *state* information from those websites. Online services like Google will have their own records of your history, both as part of the way they integrate your various online activities and through the functionality of website usage analyzers that might be installed in the code of the sites you visit.

Some of that data will be anonymized, making it impossible to associate with any one user, and some is, by design, traceable. A third category is *meant* to be anonymized but can, in practice, be decoded by third parties and traced back to you. Given the right (or wrong) circumstances, any of that data can be acquired by criminals and used against your interests.

E-commerce and Social Media Account Data

Everything you've ever done on an online platform—every comment you've posted, every password you've entered, every transaction you've made—is written to databases and, at some point, used for purposes you didn't anticipate. Even if there was room for doubt in the past, we now know with absolute certainty that companies in possession of massive data stores will *always* seek ways to use them to make money. In many cases, there's absolutely nothing negative or illegal about that. As an example, it can't be denied that Google has leveraged much of their data to provide us with mostly free services that greatly improve our lives and productivity.

But there are also concerning aspects to the ways our data is used. Besides the possibility that your social media or online service provider might one day go to the "dark side" and abuse their access to your data, many of them—perhaps most infamously, Facebook—have sold identifiable user data to external companies. An even more common scenario has been the outright theft of private user data from insufficiently protected servers. This is something that's already happened to countless companies over the past few years. Either way, there's very little you can do to even track, much less control, the exciting adventures your private data may be enjoying—and what other exotic destinations it might reach 1, 5, or 10 years down the road.

Government Databases

National and regional government agencies also control vast stores of data covering many levels of their citizens' behavior. We would certainly hope that such agencies would respect their own laws governing the use of personal data, but you can never be sure that government-held data will never be stolen—or shared with foreign agencies that aren't bound by the same standards. It also isn't rare for rogue government agencies or individual employees to abuse their obligations to you and your data.

Public Archives

The Internet never forgets. Consider that website you quickly threw together a decade ago as an expression of your undying loyalty to your favorite movie called...wait, what was its name again? A year later, when you realized how silly it all looked, you deleted the whole thing. Nothing to be embarrassed about now, right? Except that there's a good chance your site content is currently being stored and publicly displayed by the Internet Archive on their Wayback Machine (`https://archive.org/web/web.php`). It's also not uncommon for online profiles you've created on social networking sites like Facebook or LinkedIn to survive in one form or another long after deletion.

The Dark Web

As we'll learn in Chapter 6, "Encrypting Your Moving Data," information can be transferred securely and anonymously through the use of a particular class of encrypted connections known as a *virtual private network* (VPN). VPNs are tools for communicating across public, insecure networks without disclosing your identifying information. That's a powerful security tool. But the very same features that make VPNs secure also give them so much value inside the foggy world of the Internet's criminal underground.

A popular way to describe places where you can engage in untraceable activities is using the phrase "dark web." The dark web is made up of content that, as a rule, can't be found using mainstream Internet search engines and can be accessed only through tools using specially configured network settings. The private or hidden networks where all this happens are collectively known as Darknet. The tools used to access this content include the Tor anonymity network that uses connections that are provided and maintained by thousands of participants. Tor users can often obscure their movement across the Internet, making their operations effectively anonymous.

Tor is actually an acronym that stands for "The Onion Router." The many layers that make up an onion are an effective way to visualize the Tor protocol. Tor-based data can be transmitted across a network in the form of browser requests, for instance. A request can be encrypted in a way that permits each network node it visits to "peel back" only a single layer of encryption, exposing just enough information to direct the data to the next step along its path. The request is only fully decrypted once it reaches its final destination.

Tor is best known for allowing for anonymous browsing sessions—something designed to protect the identity of server clients. However, server identities can be similarly protected using what's known as *hidden services* (or, more often, *onion services*). When both clients and servers are using Tor, you can achieve true end-to-end encryption. Onion servers are identified by a string of 56 characters followed by .onion.

Like VPNs, the dark web is often used to hide criminal activity, but it's also popular among groups of political dissidents seeking to avoid detection and journalists who communicate with whistleblowers.

A great deal of the data that's stolen from servers and private devices eventually finds its way to the dark web.

What Are My Responsibilities as a Site Administrator?

Besides the moral obligation to protect your users and organization from harm, you will probably also need to ensure that your infrastructure configurations meet legal and regulatory requirements. One particularly prominent set of laws is the European Union's General Data Protection Regulation (GDPR). The GDPR affects any organization that processes data that's either sent to or from the European Union (EU). Failure to appropriately protect the privacy and safety of protected data moving through EU territory can result in significant—even crippling—fines.

Other regulatory systems that might, depending on where and how your organization operates, require your compliance include the Payment Card Industry Data Security Standards (PCI-DSS) administered by major international credit card companies and the U.S. government's Health Insurance Portability and Accountability Act (HIPAA).

Besides addressing your regulatory requirements, it's worthwhile thinking about the real-world consequences of failing to effectively protect your users' data. The impact of breaches, outages, and data loss events can go far beyond financial damage. It's not at all uncommon for clients and users to suffer permanent personal, social, health, or even ecological damage from IT disasters.

Can Escaped Genies Be Forced Back into Their Bottles?

Well, let me ask you this: have *you* ever successfully returned a genie to its bottle? I thought so. Unfortunately, it would probably be just as impractical to even try to find and delete all copies of stolen data that's been spread across an unknown number of sites—including some on the dark web.

Even getting private references removed from search engine results can involve a long, uphill struggle with no guarantee of success. Thanks to the GDPR, European residents can request help from Google using the Personal Information Removal Request Form. But you can never be sure how that will turn out, and sometimes submitting your request can make things worse. Considering taking down an offending website. Are you sure you even know how to find all the copies? Are you aware, for instance, that the Internet Archive project (https://archive.org/web), as of this writing, hosts historical versions of more than 772 billion web pages? I've actually used the project to recover lost data from 15-year-old iterations of my own sites.

What Can I Do as a User?

Here's a good place to start: think carefully before posting anything on an online platform. Are you revealing too much about yourself? Will you be comfortable having your future employers and grandchildren read this 10 or 20 years from now? Try to anticipate the places your content might end up and what value it might have for people you've never met—people unconstrained by ethical concerns who care only about making money.

Be realistic about your data. Don't assume that the contacts with whom you share files and information will be the only ones to see them. Even if your own accounts will remain secure, theirs might not. And who says those friends or colleagues will respect your privacy preferences indefinitely?

Never assume the file storage or sharing platform you're relying on won't change their privacy rules at some point in the future. Or, even better, that they'll never decide to sell your data to someone else.

Finally, here's one that makes a ton of sense and is absolutely obvious. But not only am I sure you've never done it, I'm confident that you probably never will. Remember those check boxes you're required to click before you can open a new online account? You know, the ones that say something like this:

"I have read and accept the terms of the privacy policy."

Well, have you ever actually read through one of those documents before clicking? Me neither. I mean, Google's Privacy and Terms document (`https://policies.google .com/privacy?hl=en`) is around the same length as this chapter (and not nearly as much fun). Who's got the time? On the other hand, reading it from start to finish would probably give you important insights into the real-world consequences of using Google services. It might even convince you to change the way you use the product. And reading the privacy documents for *all* the platforms you use would undoubtedly make you a better and safer consumer.

But we all know that's not happening, right?

Establishing Authenticity

You've got a strong and active interest in distinguishing between what's real and what's fake in your digital life. Considering how much unreliable content is out there, making such distinctions might not be so simple. Many of the choices you make about your money, property, and attitudes will at least partly rely on information you encounter online, and you certainly don't want to choose badly. So, here's where we'll talk about ways you can test and validate content to avoid being a victim.

Think About the Source

Always carefully consider the source of the information you want to use. Be aware that businesses—both legitimate and not—will often populate web pages with content designed to channel readers toward a transaction of some kind. The kind of page content that'll inspire the most transactions is not necessarily the same as content that will provide honest and accurate information. That's not to say that private business websites are always inaccurate—or that nonprofit organizations always produce reliable content—but that you should take the source into account.

With that in mind, I suggest you're more likely (although by no means guaranteed) to get accurate and helpful health information, for example, from the website of a well-known government agency like the UK's Department of Health and Social Care or an academic health provider like the Mayo Clinic (`www.mayoclinic.org`) than from a site called `CheapCureZone.com` (a fictitious name, but representative of hundreds of real sites).

Similarly, you should consider the context of information you're consuming. Did it come in an email message from someone you know? Were you expecting the email? Did you get to a particular web page based on a link in a different site? Do you trust that site?

By the way, I personally consider Wikipedia to be a largely accurate and reliable information site that generally includes useful links to source material. Biased or flat-out wrong information will sometimes turn up on pages but, besides for pages covering politically controversial topics, it's rare. More often than not, problematic pages will contain warnings indicating that the content in its current state is being contested. And if you do find errors? Fix 'em yourself.

Be Aware of Common Threat Categories

Spam—unsolicited messages sent to your email address or phone—is a major problem. Besides the fact that the billions of spam messages transmitted daily consume a fortune in network bandwidth, they also carry thousands of varieties of dangerous malware and just plain waste our time.

Your first line of defense against spam is to make sure your email service's spam filter is active. A spam filter will scan all incoming emails for content and language that suggests it's not something you would normally want to read. Good filters will pay particular attention to dangerous file attachments and links to dangerous Internet sites. When a message is categorized as spam, most filters will move the message to a special spam folder, where you could examine it for yourself or just delete it. Occasionally, a false positive will inadvertently send an important email to the spam folder. So, you should take a look every now and then.

Your next step: educate yourself about the ways spammers use *social engineering* as part of their strategy.

Spoofing involves email messages that misrepresent the sender's address and identity. You probably wouldn't respond to an email from suspiciousguy@darkw3b.com, but if he presented himself as e.musk@tesla.com, you might reconsider. At the very least, recognize that email and web addresses can be faked. Organizations using DomainKeys Identified Mail (DKIM) to confirm the actual source of each email message can be effective in the fight against spoofing.

Phishing attacks—which are often packaged with spoofed emails—involve criminals claiming to represent legitimate organizations like banks. A phishing email might contain a link to a website that looks like it belongs to, perhaps, your bank but doesn't. When you enter your credentials to log in, those credentials are captured by the website backend and then used to authenticate to the actual banking or service site using your identity. I don't have to tell you how that can end.

Always carefully read the actual web address you're following before clicking—or at the very least, before providing authentication details. Spelling counts: gmall.com is *not* the same as gmail.com. Consider using multifactor authentication (MFA) for all your account logins. That way, besides protecting you from the unauthorized use of your passwords, you should ideally notice when you're not prompted for the secondary authentication method and back away.

In general, be deeply suspicious of desperate requests for help and unsolicited job offers. Scammers often pretend to be relatives or close friends who have gotten into trouble while traveling and require a quick wire transfer. Job offers can sometimes mask attempts to access your bank account or launder fake checks written against legitimate businesses.

It's a nasty and dangerous world out there. Think carefully. Ask questions. Seek a second opinion. Always remember the wise rule: "If it's too good to be true, it probably isn't." And remember, the widow of Nigeria's former defense minister does *not* want you to keep $34 million safe for her in your bank account. Really.

Summary

You are responsible for digital interactions and operations taking place using your accounts or on accounts administrated by you. You should work to prevent harm from resulting from any of that activity.

Understanding how criminals—and careless administrators—can put your data at risk is critical to learning how to protect yourself and the users you're responsible for.

Before engaging in online activity, always try to think through the possible short- and long-term consequences. Is what you're about to do likely to cause you or others harm?

Reading the privacy policy documents associated with the platforms and services you use can help you understand the threat environment you'll be using.

Always examine the context of online information: is it part of a reliable website or associated with a well-known institution?

Be aware of the kinds of threats you're likely to face as you go about your life on the Internet. Only by understanding what can go wrong can you hope to protect yourself and the people who rely on you.

Exam Essentials

Understand common online attack behaviors, including cyberstalking, cybermobbing, and doxxing.   Cyberstalking involves persistently pursuing an individual's online and private identity in a threatening way. Cybermobbing is the cooperation of the owners of large numbers of online social media accounts to harass an individual with whom they don't agree. Doxxers research and then publicize private information about an individual they want to harm.

Understand the kinds of personal data that are the most sensitive and vulnerable to abuse.   Your browser history, social media account activities, online e-commerce transaction information, and health records are all categories of personal data that require special attention and protection.

Understand the regulatory requirements for which you and your infrastructure are responsible. Businesses operating in the European Union must conform to the policies of the General Data Protection Regulation (GDPR). The Payment Card Industry Data Security Standards (PCI-DSS) and the U.S. government's Health Insurance Portability and Accountability Act (HIPAA) are also important standards.

Be familiar with common kinds of digital "social engineering" attacks. Spam describes unsolicited email messages sent with the goal of getting you to respond, usually by purchasing a product of doubtful value. Spoofing misrepresents the origin and sender of the email. Phishing attacks try to get you to interact with a web resource that's made to look like an actual legitimate site.

Review Questions

1. What best describes doxxing?

    A. Falsely and illegally directing law enforcement authorities toward a nonexistent crime

    B. Publicizing a target's personal contact and location information without authorization

    C. Persistent and unwanted monitoring and harassing of a target

    D. A coordinated social media–based attack against an individual involving large numbers of attackers

2. What best describes cybermobbing?

    A. Publicizing a target's personal contact and location information without authorization

    B. Falsely and illegally directing law enforcement authorities toward a nonexistent crime

    C. A coordinated social media–based attack against an individual involving large numbers of attackers

    D. Persistent and unwanted monitoring and harassing of a target

3. As an employer, which of the following are most likely to present legal liabilities for you and your organization? (Choose two.)

    A. Threatening comments posted by your employees on your organization's website

    B. Threatening comments posted by your employees on their own social media accounts

    C. Criminal activity (like cyberstalking) launched by an employee using public resources

    D. Criminal activity (like cyberstalking) launched using your organization's website resources (like a technical support forum)

4. Which of the following types of data should generally be considered personal and private? (Choose two.)

    A. The browser history on a user's personal computer

    B. Old social media posts

    C. A consumer's purchasing history with an online store

    D. Official records of criminal trial proceedings

5. What elements are likely to be included in your "browser history"? (Choose two.)

    A. Transcripts of recent text message conversations

    B. Passwords you've used for online application authentication

    C. Information about your computer and software profile

    D. Information about the state of a past website session

6. Why should you be conscious and concerned about any of your personal data that the owners of online services and applications might control? (Choose two.)

    A. Because you could be prevented from accessing such information on your own

    B. Because it might be stolen by third parties and mined for information that might prove damaging to you

    C. Because it might be sold to third parties or used by the services themselves in ways that infringe on your rights

    D. Because your information might change and updating remote databases can be time consuming and inconvenient

7. What best describes the General Data Protection Regulation (GDPR)?

    A. It mandates the destruction of financial and health data as soon as an organization is no longer required to retain it.

    B. It mandates the retention of financial and civil records related to European Union government activities.

    C. It mandates the protection, privacy, and safety of healthcare-related data in the United States.

    D. It mandates the protection, privacy, and safety of personal data moving through EU territories.

8. Which of these is an industry (rather than government-mandated) regulatory framework?

    A. HIPAA

    B. PCI-DSS

    C. GDPR

    D. Sarbanes-Oxley (SOX)

9. Why is it important to read an organization's privacy policy if you intend to interact with their service? (Choose two.)

    A. To better understand the security and privacy safeguards built into the application

    B. To be better able to predict the chances the organization might misuse or unnecessarily expose your data

    C. To better understand the true potential costs of using the service in question

    D. To understand how the organization might use your data

10. What best describes spoofing?

    A. Using an Internet address (URL) that closely resembles a well-known, legitimate site

    B. Misrepresenting the origin address within an email message

    C. Attempting to trick individuals into revealing private information

    D. Sending unsolicited and often dishonest email messages

11. What best describes phishing?

    A. Using an Internet address (URL) that closely resembles a well-known, legitimate site

    B. Sending unsolicited and often dishonest email messages

    C. Attempting to trick individuals into revealing private information

    D. Misrepresenting the origin address within an email message

12. What should you consider when assessing the value of online information you encounter? (Choose two.)

    A. The reputation of the source

    B. Whether the information can be verified by third-party sources

    C. The number of outbound links associated with the source

    D. The presence of proper website encryption

Chapter 2

What Are Vulnerabilities and Threats?

THE LPI SECURITY ESSENTIALS EXAM TOPICS COVERED IN THIS CHAPTER INCLUDE THE FOLLOWING:

✓ **021.1 Goals, roles and actors**

- Understanding of common security goals
- Understanding of common roles in security
- Understanding of common goals of attacks against IT systems and devices
- Understanding of the concept of attribution and related issues

✓ **023.1 Hardware security**

- Understanding of the major components of a computer
- Understanding of the smart devices and the Internet of Things (IoT)
- Understanding of the security implications of physical access to a computer
- Understanding of USB devices, device types, connections, and security aspects
- Understanding of Bluetooth devices, types, connections, and security aspects
- Understanding of RFID devices types, connections, and security aspects

✓ **023.3 Malware**

- Understanding of the concepts of rootkit and remote access

✓ **024.1 Networks, network services and the Internet**

- Understanding of the concepts of cloud computing

✓ **024.2 Network and Internet security**

- Understanding of the concepts of traffic interception

- Understanding of common security threats in the Internet along with approaches of mitigation

✓ **024.3 Network encryption and anonymity**

- Awareness of cryptocurrencies and their anonymity aspects

✓ **025.2 Information confidentiality and secure communication**

- Securely handling of received email attachments

- Sharing information securely and responsibly using email cloud shares and messaging services

- Using encrypted instant messaging

The Basics: What Are We Trying to Accomplish Here?

Sometimes it's worth asking the dumb questions. And the dumber, the better. So, within the context of information technology, just what is security? I suggest that your infrastructure is *secure* when there are no people or processes with access to resources you don't want them accessing; no software services or data collections that are vulnerable to unplanned outages; no members of your technology community whose personal or professional privacy is threatened; and nothing that will be permanently lost should—through failure, theft, or malicious interference—your hardware suddenly go offline.

You could also say that a good set of security protocols ensures these four outcomes:

- **Confidentiality:** The privacy of any sensitive data and user information under your care is protected.

- **Integrity:** The intended state of your data and services is uninterruptedly maintained free of corruption and loss.

- **Availability:** The services you provide remain reliably available for on-demand requests.

- **Nonrepudiation:** Any actions executed within your IT infrastructure can be definitively traced to a recognizable author or account. This can be achieved by ensuring reliable and complete records of all system events—including associated account identities—are maintained. This is known as *attribution*.

With that out of the way, let's address some more dumb questions.

What Are Vulnerabilities and Threats?

Before we can move on to properly discuss *how* to secure your IT resources, we'll need to understand exactly what we're up against. Let's begin by defining two more important expressions: *vulnerability* and *threat*. A vulnerability is any misconfiguration, oversight, or hole in your defenses that could allow a security breach. On their own, vulnerabilities aren't necessarily a big deal. After all, even if you leave your front door open next to a busy street, as long as no one actually comes in, you're in the clear. It's a problem only if the wrong people notice.

But when it comes to digital resources, you should assume that any "open doors" will be noticed—and noticed very quickly. I myself have seen log files on new servers report intrusion attempts taking place already *less than a minute* after the initial launch. That makes a good case for building a solid understanding of that other expression: the threat.

A technology threat is any action that aims to exploit a vulnerability, whether to cause harm to your hardware or software infrastructure or to gain unauthorized access to protected data. For our purposes, this includes damage or loss resulting from user error or buggy software. From your organization's perspective, the perpetrator's good or bad intentions don't really matter.

As important as it is to understand the threats you face and how you can improve your digital defenses, it's also critical to plan your incident response protocols. For a business or organization, it's recommended to create some kind of response team with preset responsibilities and special training and resources.

The term *computer emergency response team* (CERT) is actually registered as a trade and service mark by Carnegie Mellon University. But they encourage variations of *computer security incident response team* (CSIRT) to describe such a response team.

What Can Be Exploited?

Consider this: it's quite possible that your robot vacuum cleaner has an archive of the images it used to map the inside of your home. It's equally possible that the vacuum—through its Wi-Fi connection—is in regular communication with its manufacturer. How confident are you that all that information isn't being intercepted along the way or stolen from the manufacturer's servers—or even misused by the manufacturer itself?

And consider this: by default, your smart refrigerator probably advertises itself as a network host, inviting anyone within range to come and join in with the coolness. Don't believe me? Use a mobile device to scan for available Wi-Fi networks in any residential neighborhood, and I'll bet you'll eventually see at least one network ID using the name of an appliance manufacturer. Any device with a network connection is a possible candidate for attack and exploit, and once an attacker gets inside the network, it's only a matter of time before the attack expands to other—more valuable—connected devices.

Is your smart TV set watching you more than you're watching it? Do you have any idea how much data your mobile devices are streaming outward—and who's receiving it all? Are your laptop camera and microphone being accessed by processes running without your knowledge, and do you know what's being recorded and where those recordings go? What can your smart light bulbs and connected home door locks and alarms tell the world about your home and personal behavior? Does a nasty stranger have as much—or more—control over your thermostat than you? (Could that explain why your basement is always so cold in the winter?)

With the growth of the Internet of Things (IoT), where cheap compute functionality is embedded into the design of mass-produced commercial and industrial products, a single configuration error at design time can have catastrophic repercussions down the line. Now that the sheer numbers of connected devices running worldwide has already reached the billions, there's almost no limit to the potential damage. Threat actors, for instance, have already commandeered swarms of many thousands of compromised devices and deployed their combined network and compute resources (known as *botnets*) against helpless third-party targets.

None of which is to say that more traditional PCs and enterprise servers aren't just as vulnerable to exploits. In fact, their added power and network connections make them juicier targets, and the greater complexity of their operating system environment means that they're more likely to contain vulnerabilities you've missed. The bottom line is that, if they contain silicon, they're probably open for attack. And if they're connected to the Internet, they're probably vulnerable to one kind or another of *remote execution* attack (meaning, a remote attacker who gains unauthorized access to your device and then executes unauthorized—and malicious—processes).

Who's Doing the Exploiting?

Just who are the people who most threaten your IT infrastructure? Well, *you and your organization's team members* probably present the greatest danger. That is, if you forget to back up the valuable data on an old hard drive that subsequently fails, you're the one who's responsible, right? Ditto for the USB drive that you left in your pants' pocket during its journey through the laundry.

If you'd like a frightening illustration of just how many badly configured devices there are out there, take a look at `https://shodan.io`. Shodan is a search engine that can help you find Internet-connected servers and media devices. Searching Shodan for, say, *webcam* will return information and links to thousands of connected webcams around the world. Many of those results will include links allowing you to instantly view a live feed. That's not the end of the world if the camera is aimed at the street in front of the owner's home, but if it's being used as a baby monitor, well, let's just say that people shouldn't allow passwordless access to such intimate views of their private lives.

But besides that, who are the most dangerous digital creatures out there?

- **Governments:** Law enforcement agencies can—legally or otherwise—run intrusive surveillance operations against individuals or organizations suspected of breaking the law or that oppose an agency's agenda.

- **Military Organizations:** Infiltration and attack operations—like the USB-carried Stuxnet worm first discovered in 2010—are often launched by state agencies to gather intelligence or disable functionality within computer systems run by hostile entities.

- **Corporations:** Infiltrating the IT infrastructure of an industry competitor can provide a commercial player with useful information and unfair early access to technology advances.

- **Political Parties:** Anyone who doesn't yet know that political campaigns often access sensitive information relating to their opponents simply hasn't been paying attention.

That access will, more often than not, involve illegal entry to private and protected data storage systems.

- **Scammers:** Telephone and email scam operations will often try to get you to unintentionally give up banking passwords or login access to your computer system.

- **Hackers (Black Hat):** These are individuals who discover and execute illegal entry into private and protected digital infrastructure (alternatively referred to as crackers). A *script kiddie* is someone who uses existing scripts and hacking tools to engage in cybercrimes.

- **Hackers (White Hat):** These are individuals who, for the benefit of infrastructure owners, discover and (sometimes) execute illegal entry into private and protected digital infrastructure. White hat hackers will normally alert owners and stakeholders to the existence of vulnerabilities so they can avoid loss.

Why Do They Attack?

Having at least a general picture of what attackers stand to gain from their activities can make it easier to organize your defense. "Know your enemy" and all that. Here are some common motivations.

Identity Theft

In a world where you can do most of your banking and shopping from the privacy of your own home, the credentials you use to identify yourself come to represent you at the most personal level. To a large degree, the usernames and passwords you choose become "you," and their value rises to equal everything you own.

Why would people want to steal your identity? Sometimes it's because they can use that identity to empty your bank accounts or lay claim to your property. In other cases, holding your identity can be used as leverage to force—or extort—you to behave in ways that benefit others. And it's not uncommon for a theft to serve the simple—and destructive—interest of revenge. Destroying a victim's life is, for some people, enough of a motivation.

Data Exfiltration

Whether it's a commercial competitor eager to see your secret business plans, a foreign nation's military interested in assessing your ability to defend yourself, or someone looking to steal the unfinished manuscript of the newest Sybex book (or any other copyright-protected content), if they want in, they'll have to break in. But breaking in won't be quite enough. They'll also have to find a way to get the information they found back out again so the attacker can read it.

That process is known as *exfiltration*. And you can be reasonably sure that, if you've got data worth protecting, that someone, sometime is going to give exfiltration a try on you.

Resource Destruction

You can do a lot of damage by erasing the data on someone's website server. Even if they've got backup copies of their application code and backend data, it'll still take time to put all the pieces together and relaunch the service.

For some production models, a total outage lasting only a few hours can permanently destroy the business. Imagine if a bank's website were to go offline for a few hours and then reappear with the message that customers won't be able to access their accounts for at least a week longer. Do you doubt that many customers would decide to take their banking business elsewhere?

Common Vulnerabilities

We're not going to talk about solutions here. That'll be the subject of the rest of the book. But for the rest of *this* chapter, we are going to try to better understand some of the more common vulnerabilities out there and the kinds of threats that can be used to exploit them.

Software Vulnerabilities

Whether you're a sysadmin responsible for hundreds of active devices or an end user with a laptop and smartphone, it doesn't have to take much work to keep the software you're running secure. But that doesn't mean enough people actually do it. Recovering from the chaos of an attack will often reveal that the blame lies with a remarkably predictable list of root problems.

The first—and perhaps most critical—is the presence of unpatched operating systems and software packages. Linux distributions, for instance, include repository management tools— such as ATP (Advanced Package Tool) and YUM (Yellowdog Updater, Modified)—that can be set to automatically install security updates for all active packages. While it's true that the Microsoft Windows upgrade process can sometimes be tiresome and even risky, nevertheless it would be foolish not to update your software to the latest versions whenever they become available. Such updates will, ideally, fix any recently discovered security holes. The costs of *not* patching can be catastrophic.

It should be noted that patching won't prevent *all* malware damage. After all, software vendors and anti-malware packages only protect you from threats they're already aware of. But some vulnerabilities show up without any kind of warning. Such threats are known as *zero-day vulnerabilities*.

Similarly, nation-state attackers with extraordinary access to resources and expertise will sometimes deploy what are known as *advanced persistent threats* (APTs) against very specific political, military, or commercial targets. These attacks are "persistent" in the sense that they remain quiet and undetected within large networks for long periods of time while closely monitoring ongoing activity. Once they've learned enough about their target's operations, they'll launch their malicious payloads.

Perhaps, from a security perspective, the most important individual piece of software running on a consumer PC is your web browser. Because it's the tool you use most to connect to the Internet, it's also going to be the target of the most attacks. It's therefore important to make sure you've incorporated the latest patches in the release version you've got installed and to make sure you're using the most recent release version.

Besides not using unpatched browsers, you should also consider the possibility that, by design, your browser itself might be spying on you. Remember, your browser knows everywhere on the Internet you've been and everything you've done. And, through the use of objects like *cookies* (software files containing session metadata that web hosts store on your computer so they'll be able to restore a previous session state), complete records of your activities can be maintained.

Bear in mind that you "pay" for the right to use most browsers—along with many "free" mobile apps—by being shown ads. Consider also that ad publishers like Google make most of their money by targeting you with ads for the kinds of products you're likely to buy and, in some cases, by selling your private data to third parties. So, when thinking about how you really want your private data used, it might not be too farfetched to talk about a commercial browser itself as a possible vulnerability.

You should be aware that many of your online activities can be tracked through your browsers. Allowing websites to save cookies to your computers and extract even more invasive *browser fingerprinting* information can make your website interactions more convenient. But the trade-off is the streams of data that's invisibly sent from your computer to remote services.

Privacy-focused browsers (like the Brave browser) are the most likely to block fingerprinting attempts against your computer. Unless you're willing to avoid the Internet altogether, it's unrealistic to expect perfect privacy in this context.

We couldn't leave our "greatest hits of dumb software vulnerabilities" list without mentioning those people who fail to protect their devices—especially mobile devices that are left logged into sensitive online accounts—with passwords and screen locks. Or, just as bad, those people who insist on using weak and easy-to-guess passwords. Don't try to hide. You know exactly who you are.

Hardware Vulnerabilities

What can go wrong with your hardware? Well, for one thing, all hardware will, sooner or later, inevitably fail. But that's not specifically a security issue. There are, however, a couple of things that should concern us here.

You should, for instance, protect your compute devices from physical attack. That could mean making sure the door to a server room is locked or a boot-time Basic Input/Output System (BIOS) or Unified Extensible Firmware Interface (UEFI) password is set. It could also involve establishing policies for the use of USB data sticks (which can unknowingly be used to introduce malware into a system) or installing security cameras and a protocol for viewing and archiving the video feed.

You should also regularly monitor all your server and workstation hardware components. Whether it's the computer processing unit (CPU), storage volumes, system and video memory, or network adapters: unexpected usage patterns can indicate something suspicious is going on.

For example, cryptocurrency miners (also known as *cryptominers*) enjoy illegally accessing other people's computers and running resource-intensive mining operations so they can "earn" money verifying blockchain transactions. Even if such miners aren't directly interested in damaging your property, they're certainly preventing you from taking full advantage of your resources and quite possibly running up significant usage costs.

Bioware Vulnerabilities

The elephant in the room when it comes to IT security is the *people* in the room. Everything would probably go far more smoothly if we didn't have to allow for human interference. But given that we won't be eliminating humans any time soon, you should prepare by properly educating your users (and yourself) to act responsibly around your digital infrastructure.

This includes remaining up-to-date on the latest phone and email scams that are being launched against your part of the world or your particular industry. It will also mean increasing awareness of the way you talk about your technology use in public, especially via social media posts: you never know who's paying attention. An informed technology user is a much safer technology user.

In particular, you should make sure your users understand how *oversharing* information through social media posts, emails, messaging platforms, and file sharing tools can result in harm to themselves or your organization. As we'll soon see, data and information transfers should, wherever possible, be protected by encryption and access controls. We'll talk much more about encryption in Chapters 5 and 6.

Next, I'll introduce you to some particularly serious threat categories.

Digital Espionage

As you read earlier, all kinds of people and organizations may be watching you carefully for the opportunity to get a piece of what you have. Whether it's a foreign government or some guy with a laptop parked out in front of your house, it's good to be aware of the items on the digital dinner menu they're working from.

USB Devices

Have you ever passed one of those USB flash drives lying abandoned on the sidewalk? It could be someone's wedding pictures, and you'd be doing them a big favor by plugging it in and looking for some contact information. But it could also be a booby trap loaded with malware that just can't wait to be activated and let loose on your computer.

Remember Stuxnet? That was the software worm created using the resources and ingenuity of a couple of national security agencies and used to physically destroy centrifuges being used for an Iranian nuclear program. How did the worm get so deep into the system? It was apparently carried in on a simple USB drive. So, treat stuff you find on the street with suspicion.

Backdoors

A *backdoor* is an undocumented (and, often, unauthorized) method of accessing a compute device. Device and software manufacturers might include backdoors for perfectly legitimate reasons: to give support teams a way to access and administrate a malfunctioning server, for instance. But they can also be used to let criminals in to work against the interests of the device owners.

Law enforcement organizations of a number of governments have, in recent years, sparked controversy by demanding that application developers and device makers include ways for official agencies to bypass encryption and other security protections. The idea is that criminals and terrorists have used encryption to evade detection, creating a legitimate public interest in giving governments greater power to watch them. On the other hand, since it's only a matter of time before the wrong people learn about them, the very existence of backdoors makes all computers and all software less secure for everyone—including upstanding, law-abiding citizens like you.

This isn't a debate that any one of us can resolve on our own, but you should definitely consider the possibility that the technology you're planning to use comes with one or more security compromises.

Wireless Entry Points

Times change. We live in a wireless (and virtualized) world now. Many young sysadmins will never experience the joys of pulling network cable through drop ceilings and between walls. I personally can't honestly say I miss it. But all this wireless connectivity comes with a price: anything that's more convenient for you is going to be just as convenient for someone trying to attack you. Sometimes the attack will involve an unauthorized login to one of your devices, and sometimes it'll be someone pulling data *from* your device. But either way, you don't want to leave any room for wireless misuse. Here are some technologies that will need monitoring:

Wi-Fi   Networks of local compute devices are often connected using variations of the IEEE 802.11 wireless standard. The problem is that data communicated across Wi-Fi networks that aren't secured through the use of a modern and secure encryption method is visible to any other network users. This has, over time, been the cause of significant data loss. You should be especially careful before connecting to public Wi-Fi networks.

Radio-Frequency Identification (RFID)   A small amount of data can be embedded in special tags that can then be attached to documents (like passports), retail products, tools, animals, or even people. The technology (part of the near-field communication [NFC] protocols) permits easy and inexpensive tracking of inventory and document movement, but it can also permit leakage of important and sensitive information. While progress is being made to tighten the privacy of RFID-carried data, you should remain aware of all issues related to their use.

Bluetooth   You may never have used them yourself, but I'm sure you've seen people with strange devices growing from one ear walking around and talking to themselves. They are, of course, communicating with the mobile phones in their pockets or pouches through a Bluetooth wireless connection. While at this point the technology is mature, there have historically been security concerns where outsiders have managed to include themselves in a Bluetooth connection.

Cellular Networks   Vast amounts of all kinds of data are now transmitted across the wireless networks used by cell phones. There are currently three standards of cell technology in use: third generation (3G), fourth generation (4G), and, in the process of implementation, fifth generation (5G). You should probably never consider a cellular connection completely secure and confidential. There have, in particular, been concerns about the possibility of hostile government-sponsored backdoors secretly embedded in 5G networking equipment designed for use in mass surveillance programs.

Stolen Credentials

As you've already seen, everything you are and have is often represented by the credentials you use to log into online healthcare, financial, and data services. So, you'll definitely want to protect those credentials from exposure and misuse. An important first step is to be aware of the biggest (and most frightening) threats out there.

Data Breaches

Was your credit card and account information among the millions of Target retail accounts that were exposed in an infamous 2013 data breach? How about the login credentials to your LinkedIn account; were they among the 164 million involved in LinkedIn's 2016 exposure? Or perhaps your account was one of the three billion (yes: *billion*) Yahoo accounts that were compromised in 2013 or one of the half a billion Marriott/Starwood hotel accounts hit in 2018. Worried about your credit rating? You should definitely be concerned if yours was among the 145 million accounts caught up in Equifax's 2017 breach.

   Companies of all sizes have struggled to protect their users' private data, but it's an uphill journey. As an end user of one sort or another, it's your job to protect yourself as best you can. One important step, as you'll learn later in the book, is to never reuse a single password across multiple accounts.

Your next best defense is to regularly check to see if any of your accounts have been included in real-world breaches. The most efficient way to do that is by signing up with Troy Hunt's free `https://haveibeenpwned.com` site to track the presence of your email address or passwords in known breaches. Why not head over to that site right now and check the status of your addresses and passwords?

Legal, business, and moral obligations require victims of data breaches to quickly disclose news of any attack to both regulatory authorities and impacted customers. This is critical so that effective responses can be immediately initiated to protect everyone's privacy and financial integrity as much as possible. Failure to properly disclose a breach will often lead to much greater losses of professional integrity and business stability down the line.

Identity Theft (Besides Breaches)

To a large degree, the big data breaches are out of your control: it's not your fault that some Equifax admin didn't bother patching a package on the server. But there's certainly a lot you *can* do to protect your identity from exposure. The trick is to make it harder for the bad guys to get your credentials. We're going to talk about these in much greater detail later in the book, but you should understand how to avoid the following:

Using Weak Passwords   Good passwords are long and complicated and don't reflect any knowable details about your personal life (like your birthday). Ideally, passwords should be supplemented by a form of multifactor authentication (MFA).

Phishing/Social Engineering Attacks   Scammers often use email messages, online advertisements (*adware*), or phone calls to trick people into disclosing authentication credentials. Learn how to recognize and avoid such attempts.

Open-Source Intelligence (OSINT) Breaches   Social media posts, company websites, and even job ads can reveal more than you realize about yourself and your organization. Audit what can be learned about you from publicly available information and learn how to avoid generating the kinds of information that can expose too much.

Malware

Malware (short for "malicious software") is any software that includes functionality designed to harm the target device or network. Malware packages can be introduced to a system through email attachments, by loading scripts in a browser as part of a web page (often referred to as a *trojan horse*, since, like the wooden horse sent by the Greeks besieging Troy, the dangerous script is delivered as part of what otherwise looks like a useful website), or through physical insertion via something like a USB flash drive.

Persistent rumors that malware can be transmitted by angry thoughts and insensitivity toward overworked and underpaid sysadmins are simply unfounded (but you can never be too careful).

Malware is often designed to open secondary access routes to the system that the creators can use to extract important data. A malware package might, for example, install a keylogging program that will record all of a user's keystrokes, permitting the discovery of sensitive information such as user logins and passwords. Microphones and webcams could also be hijacked, allowing full recording of events occurring in the room with the device.

Malware packages often include *rootkits*, which work automatically at the system level to protect the illegal operations from detection and removal. Rootkits can also create new backdoors, through which full remote administration sessions can be launched. These sessions can be used to fully control the host machine in order to change local software configurations and remove private data.

One particularly nasty class of malware is known as *ransomware*, where a script is used to encrypt all or much of the data on the system. When victims next try to log into the OS, they're shown a pop-up demanding a large ransom payment in cryptocurrency before the encryption will be removed. Many large business and government organizations have been hit by such ransomware in recent years, and some have been forced to pay hundreds of thousands of dollars to recover critical systems. You should, however, be aware of these important facts:

- Since we're talking about criminals, there's no guarantee that paying the ransom will actually result in regaining access.

- Some ransomware attacks can be successfully decrypted at no charge using services providing by security companies like Kasperksy (`https://noransom.kaspersky.com`).

- You can avoid the devastation and costs of most ransomware attacks by simply ensuring that your important data is properly backed up in multiple off-site archives. If you're hit with an attack, you can simply rebuild your system using your backed up data.

- Even better, you should be careful to only load online resources that you know are safe.

Cryptocurrencies are a kind of distributed, secure, and encrypted digital currency that can be used to engage in commerce without exposing your identity and important personal information. Generating cryptocurrencies requires an increased need to validate transactions by generating tokens known as *hashes*. Since generating hashes requires so much expensive and power-consuming compute time, some "cryptominers" will, as briefly mentioned earlier, hijack remote computers to use as servers, "earning" payments for the hashes they produce.

Besides that you really don't want unauthorized operations running on your equipment, the mining can consume all of your system resources *and* generate enormous electricity bills. You'll want to monitor your systems (and utility bills) for this kind of activity.

Network-Based Attacks

It's sometimes possible for outsiders to gain illegal access to your data without technically launching an "attack" at all. All they need is a presence on a network being used to transmit the files or packets without encryption. Since unencrypted data is sent across a network in plain text, an "attacker" could use a packet analyzer (like Wireshark) to "sniff" what's moving back and forth and rebuild it into its original format.

You certainly don't want anything to do with that kind of trouble. But there's more darkness lurking out there in your network.

Man-in-the-Middle Attacks

It's possible that individuals on a network could intercept a transmission sequence and alter some or all of the packets moving back and forth before allowing them to reach their destination. They might, for example, use this technique to misdirect a browser to a fake bank website rather than the real one and then record the login details the user enters. This kind of attack is known as a *man-in-the-middle* attack.

Denial-of-Service and Distributed Denial-of-Service Attacks

A determined attacker can bring down your website even without gaining access to the server. Denial-of-service (DoS) attacks direct a flood of resource requests at a web service, taking up so much of the server's resources, that it's got nothing left to serve legitimate clients. In 2019, for instance, such an attack was launched against the server behind the free image archive openclipart.org. The attack took the entire operation offline for months, leaving their chances of ever recovering in doubt.

Because generating enough spurious requests to successfully take down a large site can be beyond the capabilities of a single attacker, some attacks will harness third-party compute devices through which still more requests can be sent. By "third-party" I mean servers, PCs, and IoT devices that have been hijacked and turned into "zombies" that effectively become slaves to the attacker's direction. Groups of such zombies are sometimes referred to as *botnets*. When attacks incorporate such grouped resources, they're known as DDoS attacks.

Denial-of-service attacks can be blocked using clever firewalling techniques. Large cloud providers have the means and expertise to offer enterprise-strength DDoS protection. Amazon Web Service's AWS Shield is one good example.

Network Routing Attacks

Computer networks are run on a complex set of routing rules. How, when, and where a particular packet will be sent is determined by established protocols like the Transmission

Control Protocol/Internet Protocol (TCP/IP), the Address Resolution Protocol (ARP), and the Dynamic Host Configuration Protocol (DHCP). But a protocol is just a protocol, and there's always someone trying to work out new ways to fool the software that's using it.

So, be on the lookout for a whole toy box full of charming data theft terrors like ARP spoofing (where false IP address/host relationships are inserted into a network's ARP table), MAC flooding (where data can be "flushed" out of a managed network switch, exposing sensitive routing data), and switch spoofing (where an attacking device can pretend to be a trunking switch within a network and thereby gain the trust of legitimate network switches).

Cloud Computing and Digital Security

At its core, cloud computing is really nothing more than using the compute, networking, and storage resources of a remote platform rather than your own for your applications and data. The key structural difference is that cloud platforms normally bill on a pay-as-you-go basis, while you're on the hook for significant up-front costs for your local deployments.

My *AWS Certified Cloud Practitioner Study Guide* book (co-authored with Ben Piper and published by Wiley/Sybex) includes a more complete introduction to how cloud computing works. Within the context of *this* book, I would point out that the big cloud providers like Amazon Web Services (AWS) and Microsoft's Azure have the money and experience to handle security and reliability just as well as you—and likely a lot better.

You should be aware of a number of cloud service paradigms.

- *Infrastructure-as-a-service* (IaaS) tools like AWS Elastic Compute Cloud and Azure compute services provide virtual versions of traditional bare-metal servers. IaaS services allow you to rent the use of compute units at any scale necessary. You are responsible for maintaining the operating system and any software packages running on your server instances.

- *Platform-as-a-service* (PaaS) offerings provide a carefully defined and curated base resource stack that can simplify your own application deployments. Examples of PaaS platforms include the AWS Elastic Beanstalk service, where you upload the code for a new application and the OS and other software requirements are provided and managed by the platform.

- *Software-as-a-service* (SaaS) utilities typically deliver services to end users. Google's Workspace, for instance, provides organizations with a full managed suite of email, document sharing, and business communication tools.

Summary

Technology security ensures that your IT resources are protected from unauthorized access and your users' privacy is maintained.

Secure IT practices include being informed about existing and emerging threats as they relate to software, hardware, and various methods used by email or telephone scammers.

Badly configured networks and Internet connections are responsible for many—if not most—serious attacks causing data loss.

Even a basic understanding of the kinds of malware threats you're likely to face can help you adjust your online behavior to more effectively protect yourself.

Exam Essentials

Define *vulnerability* and *threat*. An IT vulnerability is a software or hardware state that, if exploited, would allow dangerous and unauthorized access to your infrastructure. A threat is any possible exploit of a vulnerability.

Understand the "big picture" of the security landscape. It's important to know what kinds of devices can face threats, who has an interest in attacking you, and what they would like to accomplish.

Be familiar with the major threat categories. Threat actors are likely to be after one of these three goals: identify theft (probably leading to some kind of property theft), data exfiltration, and resource destruction.

Be familiar with common software vulnerabilities. Never run devices with unpatched and out-of-date software installed. This is especially true for any web browsers you're using.

Understand the tools and vulnerabilities used by digital spies. Hostile spying attacks can utilize cheap mobile storage devices (USB flash drives), existing hardware or software backdoors, and badly configured wireless networks to penetrate your networks and access your resources.

Understand how vulnerable users' identities are in a connected world. Many of the credentials you use to access online and even local services are likely to be compromised either by data breaches of service providers or through careless exposure of private information.

Understand various categories of malware. You should understand how malware threats such as trojan horses, keyloggers, rootkits, and ransomware work (and, of course, how you can protect yourself).

Understand the basic principles of cloud computing. Many, if not most, software applications are currently hosted on platforms owned by public cloud providers like AWS and Azure. IaaS, SaaS, and PaaS are three of the most common deployment models in use within cloud environments.

Understand various categories of network-based attacks. Network transmissions can be disrupted by man-in-the-middle attacks, public-facing services can be effectively shut down by denial-of-service attacks, and the data sent through network routing tools can often be exposed to unauthorized eyes.

Review Questions

1. Which of the following are among the primary goals of well-designed information security protocols? (Choose two.)
   A. Cost savings
   B. Nonrepudiation
   C. Application efficiency
   D. Confidentiality

2. Which of the following goals is focused on tracking the origins and authors of all processes run within an IT environment?
   A. Network firewalling
   B. Application availability
   C. Nonrepudiation
   D. Malware detection

3. Within the context of IT security, what best describes a "vulnerability"?
   A. A hole in your software or physical defences that could allow a security breach
   B. An action that aims to cause harm to your hardware or software infrastructure
   C. A data store containing sensitive and hard-to-replace information
   D. An external entity with an incentive to disable your IT infrastructure

4. Which of the following best describes the Internet of Things (IoT)?
   A. Compute devices issued private network IP addresses.
   B. Mass-produced networked compute devices that regularly exchange data.
   C. Multiple simple systems combined as part of the operation of complex environments (like cars or buildings).
   D. It's just a fancy way of describing the Internet.

5. Which of the following are common motivations behind DDoS attacks? (Select two.)
   A. Data exfiltration
   B. Network connection disruption
   C. Resource destruction
   D. Identity theft

6. What is the most significant and common potential vulnerability that could be associated with an unpatched web browser? (Choose two.)
   A. The use of untrusted websites
   B. The use of weak and overused passwords
   C. Unauthorized access to your system resources
   D. The unexpected visibility of your browsing history and data

7. What measures can you take to control physical access to your servers? (Select two.)

 A. Set appropriate firewall rules on your network.

 B. Set a BIOS/UEFI password.

 C. Install secure locks to the rooms where computers are running.

 D. Ensure the hardware you're using is recent and up-to-date.

8. For which of the following software packages are you responsible for applying regular patches? (Select three.)

 A. Web browsers

 B. PC operating systems

 C. Online software services

 D. Mobile device operating systems

9. What can be done to reduce your organization's exposure to external attack? (Select two.)

 A. Train your team about the latest phishing scams.

 B. Train your team to watch for strange behavior among their colleagues.

 C. Train your team on the effective use of your business applications.

 D. Train your team about responsible use of social media.

10. Which of the following technologies could be vulnerable to exposure of your private and sensitive data through rogue wireless sniffers? (Select two.)

 A. RFID tags

 B. USB storage devices

 C. 4G mobile network devices

 D. Ethernet

11. Which of the following best describes a "backdoor" vulnerability?

 A. An undocumented method of accessing a compute device

 B. An unadvertised Wi-Fi host network

 C. A server without a password protecting its BIOS/UEFI boot process

 D. A server protected by an unconfigured firewall

12. Which of the following is a justification used by public security agencies for maintaining access "backdoors" in all mass market computing devices?

 A. To ensure that all legitimate server activities are properly secured

 B. To prevent organized criminals from blocking government surveillance of their illegal activities

 C. To properly secure both ends of all connections between consumer devices and government servers

 D. To monitor bugs and vulnerabilities in mass market devices

13. Which of the following are important and practical steps in protecting you from the impact of large public credentials leaks? (Choose three.)

    A. Use a password vault to generate and safely store strong passwords.

    B. Avoid using online e-commerce and banking sites.

    C. Never reuse passwords across multiple accounts.

    D. Regularly monitor online collections of leaked password/email combinations.

14. How are "phishing attacks" used as part of credential theft?

    A. Phishing attacks use AI-generated data snippets to penetrate a network's outer defenses.

    B. Phishing attacks flood target accounts with possible login/passwords until they chance on the right combination.

    C. Phishing attacks can fool targeted users into revealing personal information to dangerous people.

    D. Phishing attacks sniff network packets and attempt to rebuild credential sets from the captured data.

15. In what ways are OSINT breaches different from phishing attacks? (Select two.)

    A. OSINT efforts involve physical access to your compute environment while phishing can be executed remotely.

    B. OSINT breaches occur among publicly available sources, while phishing attacks target information from private sources.

    C. OSINT is a counter-crime process and is not an attack at all.

    D. Technically, OSINT gathering doesn't require the breaking of any privacy laws, while the act of phishing is, generally, criminal.

16. Which of the following best describes "ransomware"?

    A. Malicious software quietly disables local anti-malware software running on the victim's computer.

    B. Malicious software is surreptitiously installed on a computer where it proceeds to delete the local data.

    C. The victim's computer is breached, and all or much of its data is encrypted, denying the owner access.

    D. Cryptocurrency mining operations are surreptitiously run on the victim's computer, using local power and compute resources.

17. Which of the following are effective in combating ransomware attacks? (Select two.)

    A. Maintaining complete and up-to-date backups of your critical data

    B. Signing up for online ransomware prevention services

    C. Carefully following the on-screen instructions sent by the ransomware authors

    D. Working with online and law enforcement organizations to decrypt your impacted data

18. Which of the following can be used by criminals in direct support of their distributed denial-of-service (DDoS) attacks? (Select two.)

    A. Artificial intelligence software designed to explore infected systems looking for valuable data

    B. Badly designed Internet of Things networks

    C. Scripts built to destroy remote file systems

    D. Network-connected compute devices with poorly configured access and authentication settings

19. Which of the following are attack methods aimed specifically at network protocols? (Select two.)

    A. ARP spoofing

    B. MAC flooding

    C. Phishing

    D. Social engineering

20. In IT security terms, what is a zombie?

    A. A firewall that's configured to misdirect network traffic for illegal purposes

    B. A compute device whose resources have been hijacked as part of an attack against a third party

    C. A compute device whose operating system has failed, leaving it in a permanent state of sleep

    D. A human administrator who logs out of a server console without authorization

Chapter 3

Controlling Access to Your Assets

THE LPI SECURITY ESSENTIALS EXAM TOPICS COVERED IN THIS CHAPTER INCLUDE THE FOLLOWING:

✓ **023.1 Hardware security**

- Awareness of Trusted Computing

- Understanding of USB devices devices types, connections, and security aspects

✓ **023.2 Application security**

- Understanding of common types of software

- Understanding of various sources for applications and ways to securely procure and install software

- Understanding of updates for firmware, operating systems, and applications

- Understanding of sources for mobile applications

- Understanding of common security vulnerabilities in software

- Understanding of the concepts of local protective software

✓ **023.3 Malware**

- Understanding of common types of malware

- Understanding of virus and malware scanners

- Awareness of the risk of malware used for spying, data exfiltration, and address books copies

✓ **025.1 Identity and authentication**

- Understanding of the concepts of digital identities

- Understanding of the concepts of authentication, authorization, and accounting

- Understanding of the characteristics of secure passwords (e.g., length, special characters, change frequencies, complexity)

- Using a password manager

- Understanding of the concepts of security questions and account recovery tools

- Understanding of the concepts of multifactor authentication (MFA), including common factors

- Understanding of the concepts of single sign-on (SSO) and social media logins

- Understanding of the role of email accounts for IT security

- Understanding of how passwords are stored in online services

- Understanding of common attacks against passwords

- Monitoring personal accounts for password leaks (e.g., search engine alerts for usernames and password leak checkers)

After working through the first couple of chapters, you should be pretty clear about the kinds of threats that you and your digital infrastructure face. Now it's time to get down to the serious business of protecting yourself. There are, in the big picture, two parts to this protection. *Prevention* involves hardening your defenses to keep the lurking monsters out. *Mitigation* is the fine art of limiting the scope of a successful attack and reducing the actual harm that's done.

The remaining chapters of the book will cover those two themes. Prevention, you'll learn, is designed to make it harder for the wrong people to do the following:

- Get their hands—or eyes—on your equipment.
- Acquire and read the contents of your private data.
- Insert themselves into your private network connections.

Mitigation, on the other hand, ensures that you won't lose everything even if the enemy does get past the gate. For this, you'll do the following:

- Configure full, regular, and reliable data backups.
- Install internal monitoring systems that will alert you to intrusions.
- Design your system with the highest possible resource isolation.

Controlling Physical Access

We'll begin with the most obvious protection of all: making sure your hardware remains secure and under your complete control. To get you there, this chapter will cover the things you should do to protect your compute activities, the ways passwords should (and should not) be used for effective authentication, how you can fine-tune who gets access to which individual resources on your systems, how you can control the way your resources are accessed through network connections, and how to fix problems introduced by using third-party software packages.

Understanding Your Devices

Before learning to protect your physical compute infrastructure, it's probably worthwhile to spend a few moments making sure you clearly understand the basics. By "basics," I mean the core components that make up an actual computer. After all, you can't properly protect what you don't understand, right?

How Compute Works

The "compute" part of a computer is the central processing unit (CPU). This is the device that actually executes most of the arithmetic, input/output, logic, and control operations needed to make stuff happen. For most of us, the only thing we have to know about CPUs is how quickly and efficiently they can execute on behalf of the applications we want to run. So before making a purchase decision, we'll read up on processor speed (measured in gigahertz [GHz]), number of cores (eight is nice to have these days), and architecture (32- or 64-bit—although 32-bit hasn't been all that useful for a very long time).

What do CPUs have to do with security? As it turns out, much more than most of us would have guessed even a few years ago. Recently discovered vulnerabilities (like Spectre and Meltdown) in some high-end Intel chips, for instance, have been shown to potentially expose private data on a server to unauthorized access. Depending on your workload, cautious and responsible admins may adapt the way they use their CPUs in production environments.

How Memory Works

The primary resource used for storing application data as it's being used by your system is random-access memory (RAM). By and large, the faster and more reliable your RAM modules are—and the more of it you have installed—the better performance you'll enjoy from your computer. Are there any RAM-based security threats? Unfortunately, there are. It can, for instance, be possible to retrieve session data from a RAM module by booting it to a second OS. This is known as a *cold boot attack*. It's also sometimes possible to access sensitive data through the contents of a system's swap file.

Data that's meant to be persistent isn't stored on RAM modules or even in virtual memory SWAP files, but in permanent partitions on physical storage drives. Such drives might use magnetic media to store your data or, more recently on faster and denser solid-state media. Considering that pretty much all the digital data created and consumed throughout the world is stored on a drive of one kind or another, maintaining physical security for your devices is a significant responsibility.

How Storage Works

What may not always be obvious is the need to worry about your storage drives even once you're done with them. Just because they're too slow or haven't got the capacity to meet your current needs doesn't mean that someone, somewhere won't be motivated to plug it in to see if there's anything of value. Studies have shown that an alarming number of discarded and after-market drives contain undeleted data.

How Peripherals (Might Not) Work

If all that hasn't raised your blood pressure, just consider the fact that even your keyboard and mouse might be spilling your secrets for the world to see. Proof-of-concept attacks have managed to record the activities of wireless peripherals. And I'm not even going to mention the problem of network printers. Except that I just did mention it. So sorry.

Understanding Trusted Computing

Many hardware manufacturers now ship computer motherboards with a microcontroller known as a Trusted Platform Module (TPM). These modules can be used to prevent non-trusted software from running or even booting on the system. The goal was to protect users from dangerous software using a platform that, because it's immutable, cannot itself be corrupted by malware.

However, the technology hasn't always been well received. There are concerns that a TPM platform could itself be designed to undermine the privacy and reliability of legitimate systems. TPM has also prevented important software—like some Linux releases—from being installed in the first place. And TPM is sometimes seen as limiting the control users have over their own hardware.

The way you interact with TPM should reflect your specific needs and risk assessments.

Protecting Your Devices

Everything that happens on the devices you own should happen because you want it to. Processes should execute only because you stand to gain from the results. Data should be written and read only when it furthers your goals. Accounts should exist only for the users you want to be there.

But is there any way to ensure that yours are really the goals being served on your machines? Besides the obvious stuff like not leaving your phone or laptop in unprotected spaces (like an unlocked car) and restricting entry to buildings and rooms containing expensive servers, here are some other important considerations.

Who Else Is Watching?

Have you spent some happy time productively clicking away on your keyboard over the past few hours? Did you type in passwords or other sensitive information during that session? Was anyone watching? No? Are you absolutely sure about that? You might be surprised how often "shoulder surfers" quietly wander around behind computer users in an office or other public setting, subtly watching and noting your login and password information.

But you should be even more concerned about the possible presence of surveillance cameras. There has been no shortage of frightening reports involving the use of cheap and easy-to-hide wireless cameras over the past years. They've been found installed within sight of point-of-sale (POS) terminals (perfectly positioned to capture your fingers as you enter a credit card PIN) and in hotel rooms (perfectly positioned to capture *everything* you do).

Unfortunately, you need to be worried about all those possibilities, remaining constantly aware of your environment, who might be traveling through it, and what devices might be illegally watching you. Periodic glances around the room won't hurt, and visually scanning a new room for suspicious-looking devices at ceiling level is also a good idea.

But even if you're all alone in your own home and you know there are no rogue cameras installed, you're not off the hook yet. If there's keystroke logging software installed on your OS, everything you type—including banking passwords—may be recorded and transferred to just about any place on the planet. Such software could, in theory at least, come installed on new factory-provided systems. But it may also be installed later by any hacker who has enjoyed even the briefest access to your unprotected system.

There are, in general, three steps to protecting yourself from keystroke loggers (or from keyboard tracking, as it's sometimes known):

- Carefully guard access routes to your computer. If they can't get to it, they won't be able to install anything.

- Install and properly configure anti-malware software and make sure it's set to scan for keyboard loggers.

- Whenever possible, use only an OS that was built by installing a clean copy onto a properly sanitized, empty storage volume. This will obviously be much easier if your OS is one version or another of Linux.

Finally, protect your devices whenever you step away by locking your screen and requiring a password to unlock it. Once you get in the habit, it'll be painless.

The Problem with USB Devices

Portable storage devices (also known as *flash drives* and *data sticks*) using the Universal Serial Bus (USB) standard are great for inexpensively and conveniently moving relatively large amounts of data from place to place. Unfortunately, they're also great for inexpensively and conveniently moving relatively large amounts of data from place to place. The "unfortunate" bit is due to how easy it is for someone to use such a device to do some serious damage when it's plugged into someone else's computer.

Perhaps the easiest USB attack to execute makes use of a Live Linux session. Many Linux distributions allow you to write the OS image to a USB drive in a way that, when you boot a computer with the drive plugged in, you're given the option to "try Linux without installing." Such a live session gives you a fully functional Linux experience without needing to touch the software installed on the machine's main data drive. Live sessions can be great for diagnosing and fixing problems with nonbooting computers, but they can also be used to access and manipulate the contents of existing drives without having to authenticate.

The only way to reliably protect your data drives from such access is to encrypt their contents—which we'll discuss in Chapter 5, "Encrypting Your Data at Rest." Of course, as you'll learn in that chapter, encryption can complicate some of the ways you work with your data.

You should also worry about USB devices loaded with dangerous scripts primed to execute when plugged into a computer. For that, you could enforce a policy that requires that the OS on all your systems block the use of USB storage devices. On Linux, for instance, you can blacklist USB storage-related kernel modules. Windows admins can do it through group polices, and macOS systems will often use software called Endpoint Protector.

I'll stop here for a moment and tell you a bit about myself. I'm a sysadmin, so, as you might expect, I build and maintain my own computers. Besides the fact that I deeply enjoy troubleshooting problems and playing around with unpredictable hardware, I would also be reluctant to trust my computer to a professional IT technician. Of course, most techs are completely honest and reliable. But enough of them aren't that it makes me nervous.

Let me tell you a story to explain. A quarter century or so back, I wasn't yet a professional sysadmin, so when something went wrong with one of my PCs that was beyond the range of my limited skills, I had no choice but to drag the offending box to a local computer services business. Over time I became quite friendly with the owner, and we would enjoy "shop talk" conversation as he worked on my problem.

Once, as I entered his shop on a day when he was busy with other customers, the owner looked at me, changed the music playing in the background, and winked. As he continued serving the people there ahead of me, I slowly realized that the new music playing wasn't of a genre that this particular fellow would normally have listened to. He later admitted with a smile that he'd copied the music files from the computer of a friend of mine who shared similar tastes. When? When that friend had taken *his* computer in.

It seems that the IT guy made a habit of automatically hoovering all the interesting files from drives that came into his shop and then later looking through them for anything useful. And, if you believe the steady stream of incidents reported by national and international media outlets, it seems like that IT guy is far from the only one with such habits.

If you've given your PC into the care of someone who has *even heard of* USB devices (which is to say, anyone), then, unless you know and completely trust that person, you should assume your data has been copied and malicious scripts have been installed.

Managing Authentication Through Effective Password Use

Broadly speaking, there are two kinds of programs needed to run a computer. The startup itself is managed by a class of instructions often known as *firmware*. Firmware code—like the Unified Extensible Firmware Interface (UEFI) or the older Basic Input/Output System (BIOS)—is built into computer system boards and, when a computer is turned on, is used to enumerate attached hardware, locate an available software *boot loader* installed on a boot disk, and then wake the boot loader up and hand it control. The boot loader will, as its name suggests, begin loading the operating system software that will manage system processes from that point on. The boot loader and the OS that it loads are what constitutes the system software, which is the second type of program. Figure 3.1 illustrates a typical boot process involving UEFI.

FIGURE 3.1   The stages involved in booting a (Linux) computer using UEFI

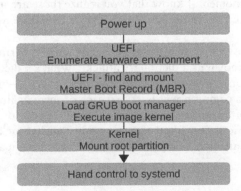

What's all this have to do with security? Well, each of those two stages—the early boot stage controlled by UEFI/BIOS firmware and the later stage managed by the OS software—can be protected by passwords. But it's important to remember that those will be *different* passwords. Setting a UEFI/BIOS password in the boot menu will effectively prevent the system from booting unless you know the password. While it is possible to reset a boot password, it'll ideally take enough time and effort to convince a bad guy to just not bother. Losing your password for the account you use to log into your OS, on the other hand, won't stop you from booting the OS; it will only keep you out of that particular account. Otherwise, the OS will run normally, and you might be able to use a separate admin account to get you back to your own data.

If your computer might find itself in places where it's vulnerable to the unwanted attention of strangers, then you'll want to lock it down with a UEFI/BIOS password. This will be the case for most laptops and other mobile devices and for kiosks that are left in public 24/7. But nearly all use cases will call for passwords on your OS accounts—and not just any password, but the kind of strong password that'll actually keep people out. The kind of password, in fact, that we're going to talk about in the next sections.

Password Policies

As a rule, operating systems and online servers won't store users' passwords in plain text. To better protect them, passwords created by users will be converted to a hash (which we'll explain in Chapter 5) and saved to a protected data file. Each subsequent time you try to log into the system and type in your password, it will be converted to a hash and then compared to the hash created when you set up the account. If the new hash matches the original, you'll be granted access to the account.

The advantage of using hashes is that, even if an intruder somehow accesses the file containing passwords, they won't be easy to use. However, even if the hashed version of your password can't be decrypted and restored to its original value, simpler password values might show up in publicly available data sets known as *rainbow tables*. For that reason, you should avoid using simple passwords.

There are three kinds of passwords, of which only one has any real security value. Let's go through them one at a time.

The first kind are passwords that are embarrassingly easy to guess. Rest assured, dear reader, that I would never suspect you of using "123456" or "pa$$word" or your birthday or pet's name. Not for a moment. I know that you realize those are no better than having no password at all. In fact, they're probably worse, since they leave you with a false sense of security.

The second category covers passwords that aren't exactly embarrassing but can easily be cracked using what's known as a dictionary attack. "What's a dictionary attack?" I hear you ask. Excellent question. It's a script that reads a "dictionary"—or a list—of thousands of popular passwords and common words, trying each of them against your account. Just about any combination of letters you're likely to think of on your own will probably be found in one of those dictionaries. To protect you against such attacks (often referred to as brute-force or dictionary attacks), many services set limits to how many wrong attempts are allowed before the account is frozen. You should consider configuring your accounts to permit only limited attempts but, better yet, choose a better password off the top.

That brings us to the third category—the one that actually works. Your own passwords should ideally be long, complex, and unique. By "unique" I mean that the password you choose for one particular account isn't in use anywhere else. Why is this so important? Because if you have an account on an online service that suffers a data breach (and they all will sooner or later), then the hackers will be in possession of the password you used along with your email address or login name. If you use that combination across multiple services, then they'll all be vulnerable. That's bad news you may not even hear about.

Based on all that, the perfect password would look something like this:

```
q34raD;fo*&Kjpoq{
```

Unfortunately, the perfect password is something that you're not likely to be able to remember. I'll address that in just a minute or two. But first I'll tell you about a different kind of perfect password. The idea is that even dictionary attacks are going to have a very hard time breaking a password that's 20 characters long. So why not put together four five-letter words like this:

```
house whale drive plain angry
```

Because there are so many letters and the words have no obvious connection to each other, it would be very difficult for any currently available computer to crack a phrase like this. But because they're all regular words, they should be relatively easy for you to remember. Consider upgrading.

When you're the admin in charge of making the rules, you can mandate that kind complexity for all of your users. You can, for instance, demand that their choices have at least eight characters made up of letters, numbers, nonalphanumeric characters, and at least one uppercase letter.

Until a few years ago, best practices recommended that you also require users to change their passwords every 30 days or so. That was then. Now we realize that forcing password changes provides very little added security and, on the other hand, leads to some nasty unintended consequences. Why is changing passwords not more secure? Well, what are the odds that a hack took place right before the previous version was set to be replaced? Not very high. What's more likely is that the password changes would occur days or weeks after the attack happened, meaning the horses will all have left the stable long before the door gets closed.

And what are those unintended consequences? Well, put yourself in the shoes of your average IT user: coming up with one password is hard enough, but what are you likely to do if you need a new one each month? How about myword5, myword6, myword7, and so on? My wife was once advised by a *manager* to vary her updated passwords based on the current month. How hard do you suppose it would be to crack those?

Still, finding the right balance between complex and easy to remember is always going to be tough. Unless you get smart.

Password Managers

The smart way to handle your passwords is by using a password manager (sometimes known as a *password vault*). At its simplest, a password manager is software that runs on your desktop, through your browser, or as an online service that lets you store authentication information in a database that's protected by strong encryption. The only way someone is going to get any useful information out of the manager is by entering the admin password. While this password should be a good one, it's effectively the last good password you'll need to remember. Any time you're prompted to authenticate for an online service or software package, you can easily copy it from your manager and paste it into the prompt. Figure 3.2 shows a cross-platform password manager. It shows how you can add and manage passwords and login information for any number of accounts.

FIGURE 3.2   A typical account entry within a password manager

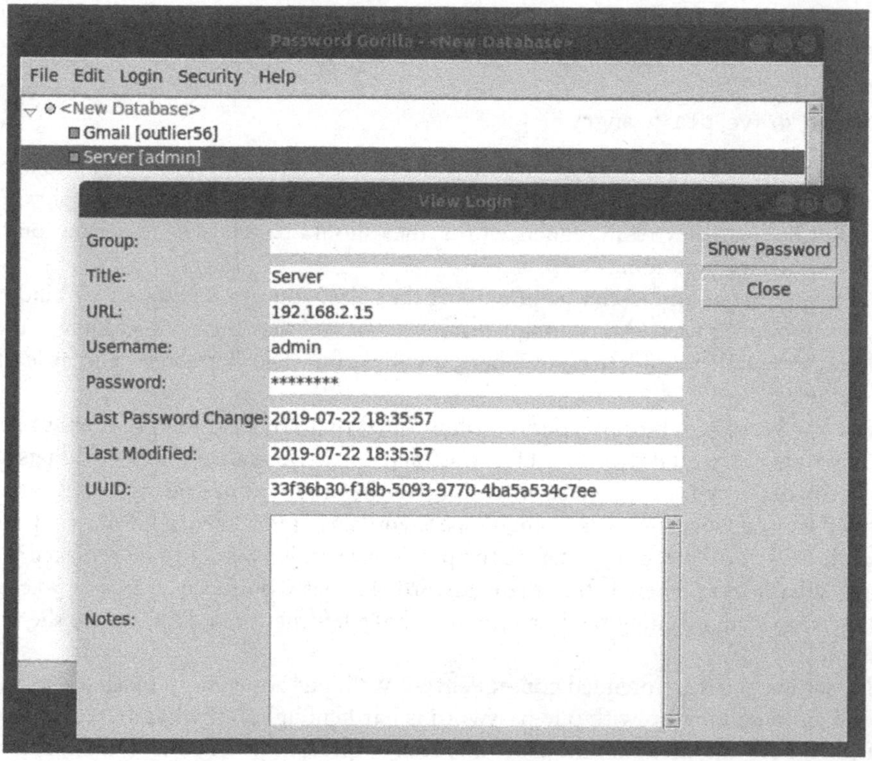

A good manager will, if needed, generate high-quality passwords for you. Some managers can also be directly integrated with web browsers. Popular managers include LastPass, True Key, and KeePass2.

Popular web browsers can also be configured to "remember" the login credentials for the many online services you might use. This can be convenient, of course, and most modern, fully patched browsers can be trusted to securely store your credentials. However, there are two potential drawbacks with relying on a browser for password storage.

- If the only copies of your passwords are the ones managed by your browser, losing access to the browser (or to the entire operating system) in the event of a software failure can be catastrophic.

- If other people have access to your user account on that computer, then they'll be able to log into any online service currently managed by the browser.

Multifactor Authentication

Passwords alone—no matter how strong—are not really enough for services that are likely to face determined attackers. The industry's preferred solution these days is to add a second authentication method *in addition to* a password. Predictably, this method is called multifactor authentication (MFA). The idea is that a login would require two or more completely independent confirmations that you are who you claim to be: something only you should know (like your password) and something only you should have (like a smartphone or a dedicated MFA device). The odds of a thief having *both* the knowledge and the object at the same time are far smaller than having only one.

How can we confirm that you're actually in possession of, say, a smartphone? The phone can be registered with your online account. Whenever you attempt to log in and provide your password, you'll also be prompted to enter a one-time passcode of some type (usually made up of six numbers). You retrieve the code, which has been sent as a text message to the phone and enter it on the login page. Protecting the passcode isn't necessary, as it usually expires after 30 seconds or so.

It is a security best practice for you and your users to enroll in MFA programs for all online service accounts that offer it. If your organization maintains its own infrastructure, you should ideally configure MFA for your accounts as well—especially accounts that are accessed through remote connections.

Monitoring for Compromised Passwords

Once a private account has been compromised, it's important to update your authentication information as quickly as possible. If you originally used a password for that account that you also used elsewhere (despite that, as we've seen, that's a bad idea), you must immediately update all other impacted accounts, too.

But there are two problems: how do you know that one of your accounts has, in fact, been compromised? And what if you have used a particular password more than once but aren't sure it's actually been exposed?

Answers to both questions can be found at Troy Hunt's Have I Been Pwned? (HIBP) website. Troy is a very highly regarded security professional who, some years ago, took it on himself to freely provide a critical service to the community. His website (`https://haveibeenpwned.com`) maintains a database of the contents of all "credential dumps" published by hackers and hacking organizations. If your email address or password was included in any of those dumps, they'll show up in searches of Troy's database (although not together, as that itself would be a huge security breach!).

As you can see from Figure 3.3, the site lets you search for your email. My "info" email address appears to be clean.

FIGURE 3.3   The results of an email search of the HIBP database

A domain search will return matches from the database for any addresses associated with a particular domain. To complete this search, you'll first need to verify that you are the owner of the domain. In addition, as Figure 3.4 illustrates, you can also search for individual passwords. This search revealed that an old password I no longer use has been compromised many times.

FIGURE 3.4   The results of a search of the HIBP database for a password string

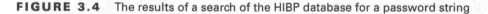

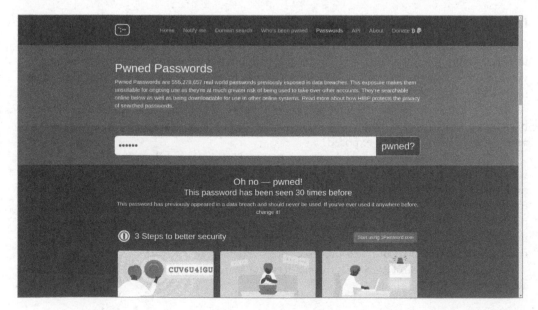

More significantly, you're also able to subscribe to updates to any of those searches so you'll be alerted whenever new breaches occur. That's definitely something you should get to right away.

Some Other Ways to Manage Authentication

Several other ways of managing authentication are particularly important and helpful.

- Single sign-on (SSO) systems permit a user to authenticate just once and gain access to multiple related services. An example of SSO is the federated logons provided by large online platforms like Google, Facebook, and Microsoft. Once you've authenticated to Gmail, for instance, you'll often have access to many other services, including My Drive and YouTube.

- One-time passwords (OTP; or, alternatively, time-based one-time passwords) are character strings that can be transmitted to a mobile device owned by someone attempting to log into a service. For instance, after entering your password for your bank's website, a numeric code—valid for a limited time—might be sent as a text message to your smartphone. Your authentication won't be complete until you've also entered that code on the website.

- Authenticator applications (like a Yubi hardware key or the software Microsoft Authenticator) are physical devices or software tools that can be used to implement OTP authentication in a way that avoids some of the shortcomings of text message-based MFA processes.

- Security questions can be used in the event you forget the password you set for a particular service. As part of the recovery process, you might be required to provide the correct answers to security questions that you set when the account was created.

- Email verification is another common account recovery tool you'll encounter. While attempting to recover access to an online account, you might, for instance, be asked to provide a character code that was sent in a message to your email account. Since you're the only person who should have access to that email account, identifying the code is seen as confirmation of your identity. This obviously wouldn't work to recover access to the email account itself.

Managing Authorization Through Permissions

Closely related to the *authentication* process is *authorization*. Where the former controls who gets into the system, the latter determines what they'll be able to do once they're in. This section will briefly explore why we implement authorization and how it works.

As the name suggests, a *multiuser environment*—like a modern operating system or cloud platform—permits multiple account users to be logged in at the same time. But it's understood that not all of those users should get equal access to system resources. After all, one might be an admin, another might only log in to access data for a related project, and a third will be there just to use productivity tools. Each of those roles will require access to a different set of resources, and you don't want any unnecessary overlap between them.

It wouldn't make sense, for instance, for office productivity suite or guest users to be able to play around with some of the core system configuration files, would it?

So, it's common to set permissions by resource, defining who should be able to read, edit, or delete a particular file or folder. An admin user would probably be given global powers, while an individual user would, by default, be able to edit only the objects belonging to that account. Rights can be assigned to a group so that any user who is a member of the group will be able to use any related resources. Figure 3.5 shows a typical permissions setup pattern.

FIGURE 3.5   Permission levels assigned to users and a user group

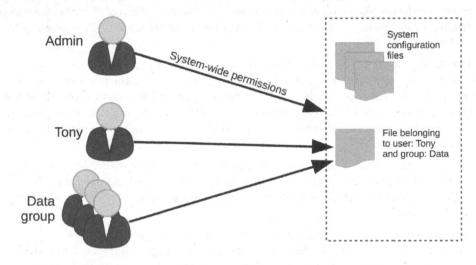

Controlling Network Access

These days, remote threats against your devices are just as common and serious as the in-person kind we've been discussing until now. That's because computers just aren't all that useful anymore without network connectivity. But of course if you can log in remotely, then you can be sure other folks are going to try to follow. To help you beef up your network defenses, this section will cover the basics of network firewalls, ways to protect yourself from network-borne malware, and how to productively apply that most uncommon of qualities for fighting the good fight: common sense.

Firewalls

A firewall is really nothing more than a tool for inspecting and filtering each data packet traveling to or from a given device. If a packet meets one or more conditions defined by your firewall rules (sometimes referred to as an *access control list*, or ACL), then it will be either allowed through or rejected, according to the terms of the rule. That much all firewalls share in common. But the way they get their work done, where they'll do it, and the architecture they'll use along the way will depend on choices you make. Let's explore some of those.

Software vs. Hardware Firewalls

Though they do pretty much the same things, a Juniper or Cisco hardware firewall can easily run you more than $10,000, while the open source OpenWRT or pfSense packages are free. So what's the difference? Well, it's not complexity: both solution categories require significant expertise to properly configure and administrate. And it's not versatility: both solution categories have all the features you'll need for any use case I can think of.

To some degree, for smaller deployments at least, it's a matter of perception. Some managers just don't *feel right* using a commodity PC running an open-source software firewall, even if their admins are for it. And one shouldn't minimize the value of software support offered by the big commercial vendors. But in some environments, the choice will be far more straightforward. If, say, you're responsible for protecting 1,000 servers from the threat of attack and your traffic is routinely measured in gigabytes per second, then your commodity PC just won't have the capacity for the task.

The solution you choose will, as always, reflect your specific needs. If you're responsible for a full-on enterprise deployment, you'll probably want a purpose-built firewall appliance. If you're working with relatively limited infrastructure and network bandwidth, a software firewall could also work. And for a stand-alone PC or laptop, you can use a firewall that comes with the OS, like Windows Defender or Ubuntu's Uncomplicated Firewall (UFW).

Local (Endpoint) vs. Cloud Firewalls

Data packets are directed from place to place within a network based on the contents of small metadata headers that were attached when the packets were first sent. The headers used by various protocols include information about the packet's initial origin, ultimate destination, and the network protocol it's using. Figure 3.6 illustrates the way a network packet can be designed.

FIGURE 3.6   A simplified illustration of the contents of a TCP data packet including metadata header information

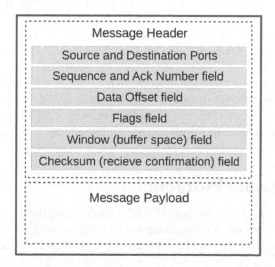

Message Header
Source and Destination Ports
Sequence and Ack Number field
Data Offset field
Flags field
Window (buffer space) field
Checksum (recieve confirmation) field

Message Payload

At each hop on a packet's journey, a network router must read its header and decide what to do next. If the destination address is local, the router could redirect the packet to that host. If, on the other hand, the destination is on a different network, then the router could forward the packet along to a router that's one step closer. But either way, a firewall running on a router must be applied to decide whether processing the packet is allowed according to local rules. If there's a problem, the packet could simply be deleted—with or without issuing a notification to the sender.

This will all work the same way wherever the firewall happens to live. Traditional operations built in a business's server room would place a firewall device at the "edge" of the local network, becoming the initial stop for all incoming traffic and the final local stop for outbound traffic. By "edge," I mean that the firewall would often be the only device plugged directly into the Internet service provider (ISP) router, with all other devices getting their Internet access *through* the firewall. Figure 3.7 shows how that might look.

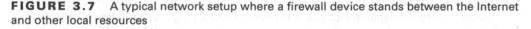

FIGURE 3.7   A typical network setup where a firewall device stands between the Internet and other local resources

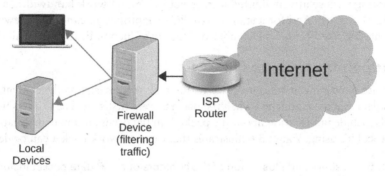

The basic structure and function of firewalls on cloud services like the Amazon Web Services (AWS) will work the same way—even if they don't necessarily call them "firewalls." AWS, for instance, names the tools used to filter traffic into and out of its compute (Elastic Compute Cloud, EC2) and database (relational database service [RDS]) services *security groups*.

An AWS security group will by default block all incoming traffic and permit anything heading out. The example shown in Figure 3.8 will permit all Secure Shell (SSH) remote login sessions using port 22 and Hypertext Transfer Protocol (HTTP) traffic using port 80 that's inbound from any source location. All other inbound traffic using any protocol or port would be rejected.

Virus and Malware Protection

What do viruses have to do with networks? Well consider that, these days at least, the vast majority of virus infections occur through network connections of one sort or another. The first virus I ever contracted—way back in the early 1990s when I was running MS DOS

FIGURE 3.8 An AWS EC2 security group permitting SSH and browser (HTTP) traffic into the resource no matter where it's coming from

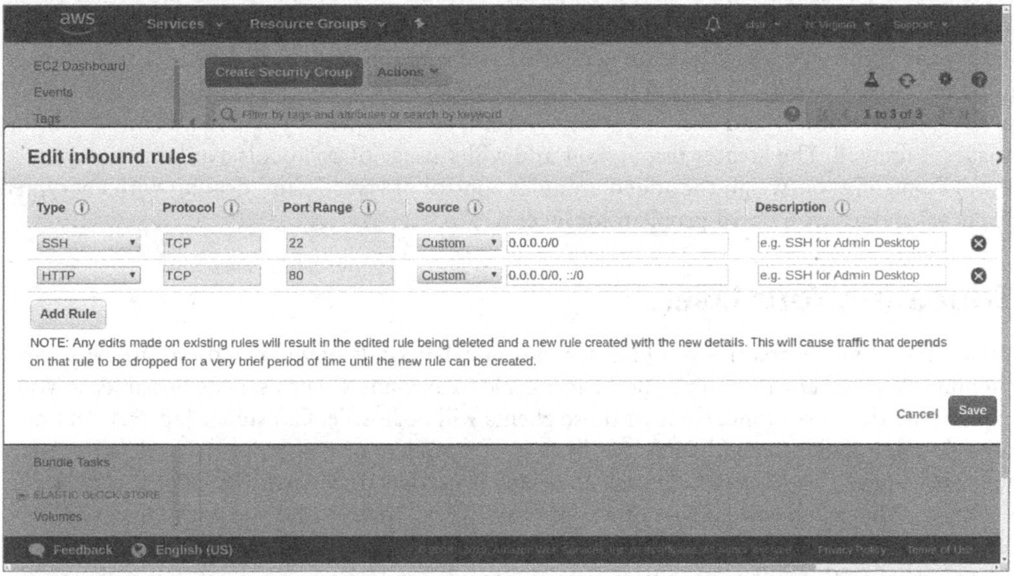

3.3—came as a "free bonus" on a software program's 5.25″ floppy disk. But when was the last time you purchased software on a disk?

So here, without further ado, is most of what you need to know about using virus and malware protection tools: acquire, install, and use them. Right now.

That'll about do it. However, there are just a few important fine-print kind of details:

- *Malware* is any script or program that's designed to perform actions contrary to the best interests and desires of an infected device's owner. Many modern browsers come with tools for blocking scripts and ads: you should use them whenever possible.

- Beware of fake antivirus software that's only pretending to protect you but, in reality, might be trying to fool you into paying for a nonexistent service (known as *scareware*) or even inserting its own malware on your system. Ensure that you only install antivirus software from reputable providers that you've acquired from reputable sources.

- Apply all recommended firmware and operating system security updates as soon as possible.

- No matter what else you do, make sure you keep your web browser patched and up-to-date.

Network Firewalls vs. Application Firewalls

Firewalls can operate at different communication layers, allowing them to filter traffic using different methodologies. A network—or layer 3—firewall (also known as a *packet firewall*) will leverage the protocols and functionality of the TCP/IP stack to filter network traffic based on source and destination IP addresses and ports. Application—or layer 7—firewalls, on the other hand, can dig beyond just a packet's header metadata and into the actual payload content. Such firewalls can control traffic using more sophisticated patterns that take into account the way it will ultimately be used at the application level. This allows a firewall to better understand the threats your applications face. While layer 7 firewalls would seem to provide greater power and accuracy, there will still be times when you should consider using a layer 3 firewall. The greater throughput and wider range of protocols available to layer 3 will sometimes outweigh the added granular control of layer 7, and dealing with encrypted application data won't be a problem for layer 3.

Educating Your Users

What kind of vulnerabilities you face depends on what kinds of workloads your devices are running. Web servers are built to be as accessible to as many client users as possible, so you can be sure that, over time, some of those clients will be hostile. Consumer laptops, on the other hand, usually access the Internet by way of a modem or router, so, using default settings, it wouldn't be so easy to launch an attack from outside the network that gets past that perimeter. The primary weakness of a consumer PC, however, is the one with fingers hovering above the keyboard.

As a rule, a PC user has to initiate some contact before malware can act. For instance, you would need to open an email from an unfamiliar sender and perhaps also click an attached file before the dangerous payload is activated. Or you would have to visit a website and load a page or click a link to start up a dangerous script.

That's exactly where education comes into the picture. If you were careful to visit only legitimate, reputable websites, then you would significantly reduce your exposure to risk. But how can you tell legitimate websites from the other sort? One important tool is familiarity with how Internet addresses are formed. The trick is to learn how to "read" the syntax used by uniform resource locators (URLs).

We'll start with a useful example: the URL on Amazon for one of my other Wiley books.

```
https://www.amazon.com/gp/product/1119982626
```

Here's how it breaks down:

- `.com` represents the top-level domain under which this website exists. Other top-level domains are `.org`, `.edu`, and, for U.S. government sites, `.gov`.

- `amazon` is the hostname of this particular domain, which exists within the `.com` top-level domain. In theory, `amazon.org` could be an unrelated domain owned by another organization. In practice, `amazon.org` is also owned by Jeff Bezos and company, and as you'll discover yourself if you point your browser to it, `amazon.org` redirects visitors to the regular `amazon.com` site. This is an important point we'll come back to later.

- "`https` in our URL example specifies the protocol your browser should use to read and display the contents of the page. Because it ends with an *s*, `https` represents a secure (encrypted) version of the HTTP protocol. If you don't use either `http` or `https` in your URL, most browsers will assume you're requesting a regular, nonencrypted HTTP.

- The "www" subdomain that precedes the `.amazon` in the URL stands for "World Wide Web." But, for the vast majority of websites, including it is optional. In fact, the man who created the World Wide Web—Sir Tim Berners-Lee—has apologized for originally including www in the protocol specification, recognizing that for years it imposed an unnecessary burden on countless millions of web users.

- Anything that follows the `/` after the hostname represents the name and location (on the web server's file system) of the file containing the web page you're reading and is often referred to as the *path*. The number `1119982626` might be the name of the file itself (that exists within the server's `/gp/product/` directory), or it could be the name of a directory containing a file whose actual name is either `index.html` or `index.php`. A URL could include further data representing details like port numbers and authentication tokens, but this will do for now.

So now, how can you use all that background to improve your network security? Here's how:

- Before logging into a site—especially an e-commerce or banking site—confirm that the URL displayed by your browser begins with `https` and not just `http`. Most browsers will also display a symbol like a green lock if the site is reliably encrypted. Never engage in any sensitive activity on a site where those are missing.

- Double-check to make sure that the hostname and top-level domain match what you'd expect. If you see `.org` for a bank or business, you should be suspicious. If you see the company name misspelled (like `ammazon.com` or `amazonbooks.com`), you should be *very* suspicious. Criminals often try to purchase and use domain names of common misspellings, and there's no knowing what they'll try to get you to do if you land on one of them.

Finally, always be aware of the context of anything you do online. Never lose sight of who it is that owns the website you're visiting and what you'd normally expect them to do. Always look at the full URL of a link in an email or on a web page before clicking. You can usually see the full URL by hovering your mouse over the link. Don't be intimidated by long addresses: you now know how to parse them.

Controlling Software Sources

As you've seen, you don't want to allow just anyone to power up and log into your devices. And you don't want to leave any unnecessary network connections open through which the wrong people can get to your digital resources. But there's still one more possible attack vector you should carefully watch: the software you use. Think about it: if a software developer wanted to include, say, a keystroke logger deep in the code for the Android media player you just downloaded, would you notice? And how long would it take for you to realize that all the banking passwords and private emails you tap into your smartphone are being recorded by that logger and sent to a remote command server somewhere for who knows what purposes?

How much do you really know about the dozens of apps, programs, and scripts you regularly use? If you're not a developer, you certainly wouldn't learn much by reading through the code. And even if you do know your way around an IDE—and the software you're looking at happens to be open source—do you really have the time and patience to methodically work through thousands and thousands of lines of code looking for bugs and malicious functionality? So, one way or the other, when you install apps on your devices, it's because you choose to trust the provider.

But is that always a good idea? The short answer is "no." The longer version is that you should insist your software providers *earn* your trust. In other works, since the health and very survival of your devices and data relies on the software you use, make sure you get your software only from reliable sources.

That's easier said than done. How *do* you go about vetting your software sources? The first step is to get out of the habit of quickly downloading and installing any apps that look interesting or fun. Instead, look for information about the developers and the repository that hosts the software. Ideally, use software only from one of a small number of centralized, official repositories. How do you identify "centralized, official repositories?" In some cases, it'll be easier than others.

PC Software Repositories

If you're running Linux, your distribution will include a software package manager that's connected to a carefully curated repository providing many tens of thousands of packages. Debian/Ubuntu users, for example, will get the Advanced Package Tool (APT) system, and Red Hat/Fedora/CentOS systems use the RPM Package Manager via either the YUM or Dandified YUM (DNF) managers. If you stick to those package managers, you can be confident that your software will be solid when you get it and will be regularly updated and patched as long as you keep it.

The Windows software scene is a bit less settled. For years, you were pretty much on your own when looking for third-party software. Your best bet was to stick with biggest and most well-known companies. In recent years, Microsoft has worked to reproduce the Linux software ecosystem experience. PackageManagement (also known as OneGet) is now shipped as part of Windows 10 and Windows Server 2016. Chocolatey is a software manager for Windows that's been around a bit longer but isn't an official part of the OS. Similarly, Homebrew is a third-party software manager aimed at macOS users. Such managers don't guarantee your software will be secure, but they certainly go a long way in reducing your risk.

Mobile Package Management

While, as long as you follow the rules, the Linux software management world is in great shape and Windows and macOS are pretty much under control, loading stuff onto your phones and tablets is a whole different thing. Official app stores for iPhone and Android are helpful, but there have been plenty of high-profile problems. And keeping even the core OS software for your Android phones in particular updated and patched is a challenge that hasn't yet been completely solved. You might make your choice of smartphone vendor and wireless carrier dependent on the ability to provide regular and timely software updates—not all carriers are equal in this respect.

Google now includes software Play Protect with the Play Store app. You should check the Play Store settings to confirm that the tool is active and that your device is "Play Protect certified."

Summary

Maintain as much control as possible over your computing environment, including the original OS installation and its physical location. This also includes ensuring that IT tech professionals you don't know and trust don't enjoy unsupervised access to your data.

Your computer can be protected by passwords at two stages: at the UEFI/BIOS boot stage and at the OS login stage. Maintaining strong passwords for both is important.

Ensure the passwords you use are long, complex, and unique. Password managers can safely store endless high-quality passwords and make them securely available to you without having to memorize them.

You log into an account using authentication credentials, but what you'll be allowed to do on that account is defined by your particular authorization—which is determined by the permissions associated with particular resources.

Antivirus and anti-malware software is, in many cases, critical for maintaining the security and functional health of your computers and mobile devices.

Always keep your web browser fully updated and patched.

Whenever possible, get your apps and software programs from reliable and official repositories.

Exam Essentials

Be aware of the ways your computer activity can be illegally monitored.   Understand how "shoulder surfers" and keystroke logging software can monitor and record your computing activity without your knowledge.

Understand how to control the use of portable storage devices.   You can use OS settings to restrict the use of USB data sticks in your organization or around your home. Encrypting storage drives on private computers can also protect you from exposure through live USB sessions.

Understand what to avoid when choosing passwords.   Passwords should be complex and difficult to predict, but, to limit your exposure to risk, they should also not be used for more than one account globally.

Understand how multifactor authentication works.   When an account is set to use MFA, you might be prompted to enter a temporary code displayed on a virtual or physical device *in addition* to your password. This leverages something you know with something you have to increase the security of your authentication.

Know how to monitor for compromised passwords and authentication information.   The Have I Been Pwned website provides access to databases of compromised credentials. You should track those databases to ensure none of your credential information has been part of a breach.

Understand how to control behavior of all system users.   By applying permissions appropriately to all system resources, individual users and group members should all be able to access only the resources they'll need to get their work done and no more.

Understand the function and purpose of a network firewall.   Firewalls can be configured to inspect the metadata of each data packet coming from outside your network. Should the metadata characteristics conflict with a firewall policy rule, the packet can be rejected.

Know how to choose the right firewall solution for your environment.   Individual PCs can use the firewalls built into the OS; small infrastructure deployments can use open source, Linux-based software firewalls; while large enterprise deployments will usually need proprietary hardware firewalls made by companies like Juniper and Cisco.

Understand how to "read" a URL.   Being able to parse a URL and separate the protocol, hostname, top-level domain, and local file address elements is an important tool in distinguishing between legitimate and dangerous websites.

Be familiar with major package managers and software repositories.   Ubuntu uses the APT package manager; Fedora uses RPM; Windows 10 users can make use of PackageManagement; and macOS can leverage Homebrew.

Review Questions

1. Which of the following best describes "mitigation"?

    A. Steps undertaken to prevent an attack against your IT infrastructure

    B. Steps undertaken to reduce the impact of an attack against your IT infrastructure

    C. Tools designed to detect an imminent attack

    D. System-wide authentication settings

2. What external devices threaten the privacy of your computer activities?

    A. Operating system bugs

    B. Software keystroke loggers

    C. Surveillance cameras

    D. Shoulder surfers

3. What is the primary risk presented by USB storage devices that can boot into live Linux sessions?

    A. Once the live session is running, the user can mount and—potentially—manipulate any attached storage drives.

    B. Live Linux sessions are inherently insecure because they require no password.

    C. Live Linux sessions are inherently vulnerable to external attacks.

    D. A live Linux USB device could contain hidden malware.

4. Which of the following carries the high risk of the unauthorized introduction of malware or spyware into your system?

    A. Connecting your compute devices to unfiltered power sources

    B. Leaving portable data storage volumes unencrypted

    C. Failing to password-protect smartphones

    D. Leaving USB-friendly computers exposed to uncontrolled access

5. How can you protect your data from unauthorized access even in the event that your computer is stolen?

    A. Configure restrictive software firewall policies at the OS level.

    B. Encrypt the data drives.

    C. Create a strong OS password.

    D. Control access to the location where your computer is kept.

6. Which of these is firmware used to enumerate its hardware environment and then find and hand control over to a boot loader?

    A. The Master Boot Record (MBR)

    B. The Unified Extensible Firmware Interface (UEFI)

    C. The OS kernel

    D. The root partition

7. Which of the following are important elements of a strong password? (Select three.)

  A. Nonalphanumeric characters

  B. A combination of upper and lowercase letters

  C. Empty spaces

  D. At least eight characters in total

8. You control the resources that will be available to individuals logged into their accounts using _____.

  A. Verification

  B. Authentication

  C. Authorization

  D. Encryption

9. What is multifactor authentication (MFA)?

  A. An authentication method that requires more than one type of information

  B. A process that submits a password string to multiple hashes to protect them

  C. A policy forcing users to employ more than one character type in a text password

  D. A software design paradigm that submits external variables to two or more checksums

10. What kind of environment would be an appropriate use case for an open source firewall solution like OpenWRT?

  A. To protect a large enterprise operation involving thousands of servers

  B. To protect the infrastructure of a small business

  C. To protect a single stand-alone computer running Windows

  D. To protect a single stand-alone computer running Ubuntu Linux

11. Which of the following routing information will commonly be found in the header metadata of data packets? (Select three.)

  A. The packet source

  B. Applicable routing rules

  C. The networking protocol being used

  D. The packet destination

12. How would you describe a script designed to perform actions contrary to the best interests and desires of a device's owner?

  A. Malware

  B. Antivirus software

  C. Firewall rules

  D. Spam

13. Which of the following is an advantage of a layer 7 (application) firewall over one operating on layer 3 (network)?

    A. Greater accuracy

    B. Wider range of protocols

    C. Greater throughput

    D. Ability to take packet source and destination into account

14. Which part of the web address URL `https://www.amazon.com/gp/product/1119490707` represents the top-level domain?

    A. `amazon.com`

    B. `https`

    C. `.com`

    D. `1119490707`

15. Of all the elements of a standard URL, which is the one that's most important for confirming that the site you're loading is secure and encrypted?

    A. Hostname (`amazon.com`)

    B. Top-level domain (`.com`)

    C. Subdomain (`www`)

    D. Protocol (`https`)

16. Considering that they're running far from your office, how can you protect your cloud servers from dangerous network traffic? (Select two.)

    A. It's not possible: you have no choice but to rely on your cloud provider.

    B. You can configure the firewall tools offered by your cloud provider.

    C. You can install and configure the same software firewalls you might use locally.

    D. Cloud providers handle all firewalling for you automatically.

17. Why is making sure that a website uses HTTPS not enough to completely guarantee that there's nothing dangerous on the site? (Select two.)

    A. Because website encryption (represented by HTTPS) isn't helpful for security

    B. Because even a properly encrypted connection could be used for malicious scripts or content

    C. Because your own browser—if not properly patched—could invisibly permit dangerous operations

    D. Because a browser could display HTTPS incorrectly

18. How can you be relatively sure that PC software packages you download and install are actually safe? (Select two.)

    A. Only use software from curated repositories (like Debian Linux's "APT" system).

    B. Only use software that comes from a website using a `.com` top-level domain.

    C. Only use software from well-known and reliable vendors.

    D. Only use software designed for business productivity and avoid games and entertainment.

19. How can you be relatively sure that the third-party software installed on your mobile devices isn't causing you harm? (Select two.)

   A. It's not a big deal: mobile providers have app security under control.

   B. Avoid unofficial app stores.

   C. Make sure your core mobile OS is patched and up-to-date.

   D. Only use productivity apps.

20. Which of the following is *not* a curated software repository?

   A. Chocolatey

   B. Homebrew

   C. SafeStore

   D. YUM

Chapter

4

Controlling Network Connections

THE LPI SECURITY ESSENTIALS EXAM TOPICS COVERED IN THIS CHAPTER INCLUDE THE FOLLOWING:

✓ **021.2 Risk assessment and management**

- Know common sources for security information

✓ **024.1 Networks, network services and the Internet**

- Understanding of the various types of network media and network devices

- Understanding of the concepts of IP networks and the Internet

- Understanding of the concepts of routing and Internet Service Providers (ISPs)

- Understanding of the concepts of MAC and link-layer addresses, IP addresses, TCP and UDP ports, and DNS

✓ **024.2 Network and Internet security**

- Understanding of the implications of link layer access

- Understanding of the risks and secure use of Wi-Fi networks

Any network, including the Internet itself, is a collection of hosts (computing devices of one sort or another) and routers (devices for forwarding data between networks) and the cables or wireless channels that connect them. The goal is to permit the transmission of data from one host to a second as quickly, securely, and reliably as possible.

Without at least a basic feel for the way networks operate, you'll have a hard time understanding the elements of network security. So, we'll start off this chapter with a high-level overview of the structure of networks themselves. We'll then learn how to effectively scan your networks for vulnerabilities and rogue devices. Finally, we'll talk about actively securing your networks, along with the devices that use them.

Understanding Network Architecture

One problem facing networks is that they're made up of hardware and software tools that are controlled by a broad range of standards. To successfully exchange data, those standards must be compatible. The standardized architectural model that's been used to make networks work since the 1970s is known as the Internet Protocol suite. The principal protocols used by the suite are the Transmission Control Protocol (TCP) and the Internet Protocol (IP). Together, they're what's referred to by the "TCP/IP" designation you'll often see referenced.

For more on those protocols, you can read their original request for comments (RFC) pages. For TCP, that would be RFC 793: `https://tools.ietf.org/html/rfc793`. And for IP, it would be RFC 791: `https://tools.ietf.org/html/rfc791`.

The Transmission Control Protocol

TCP is used by many core connectivity applications, including browsers using Hypertext Markup Language (HTML), email services, and remote session tools like OpenSSH. The protocol permits applications at either end of a connection to communicate with each other without the need to know anything about the underlying connection. TCP will establish a connection and manage it by preparing data for transmission, transmitting it, checking for errors, and sending notifications of success or failure.

TCP compatibility and functionality are usually built right into the operating system for use by software applications that use them. So, you'll rarely need to get your hands dirty with configuration. But, to properly configure firewalls or work with network troubleshooting tools, you will have to at least know which of your network applications is using TCP as opposed to protocols like the non-error-checking User Datagram Protocol (UDP) or Internet Control Message Protocol (ICMP).

The Internet Protocol

The IP protocol defines how network packets are directed between source and destination hosts. That definition covers accepted standards for the syntax used to describe Internet addresses and how those addresses are to be embedded in packet headers. At any step in its journey, a packet's header is read by routing software, which, using the TCP-compliant network infrastructure, will direct the packet onward toward its final goal. What interests us right now is the structure used by IP addresses, as that will help us understand how our networks themselves are designed. And *that* will help us understand how to best protect those networks.

Any device that's attached to a network must have some way of distinguishing itself from all other devices; otherwise, there would be no way to confidently know where traffic should be sent. The fourth version of the IP protocol—known as IPv4—established a 32-bit numerical naming system where numbers between 0 and 255 are assigned to each of four octets. A typical IPv4 address might look like this:

192.168.3.25

If you've ever taken the time to multiply $256 \times 256 \times 256 \times 256$ (where 256 is the possible numbers between 0 and 255), you'll know that you'll get a number higher than four billion (2^{32}, to be precise). This means that IPv4 addressing can provide us with a theoretical maximum usable address set of just over four billion. That sounds like a very large number. Okay, so it *is* a very large number. But when you consider how many billions of devices (like smartphones, webcams, and connected cars) are already connected to the Internet—and how many more are being added each second of every day—then you'll understand the dark and scary future facing network engineers back in the 1990s. Two successful solutions were adopted: Network Address Translation (NAT) and a new 128-bit addressing system now known as IPv6. We'll look at each of those soon enough. But first let's understand how 32-bit addressing works.

IPv4 Addressing

An IPv4 address is made up of a network identifier and a host identifier. So, for example, 192.168.1 could represent the network, which is an address space that will be shared by all devices you want to live within that isolated network. The final number to the right—say, 10—would be the unique host identifier of your laptop. Using that configuration, your network printer might be given an address of 192.168.1.20, and the Wi-Fi connection used by your smartphone when it's in the house could get 192.168.1.55. The router itself, besides being responsible for assigning addresses to your local devices and providing connectivity with the outside world, would probably have an address of 192.168.1.1. Figure 4.1 shows how such a setup might look.

FIGURE 4.1   A typical example of IP address allocations within a private subnet

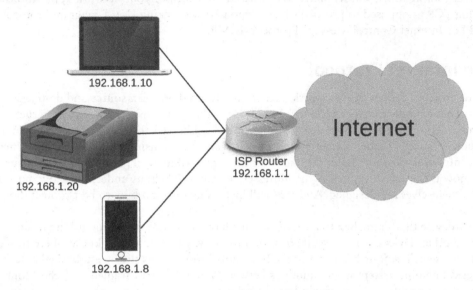

But there's a problem here, since a single address (like 192.168.1.10) could be read more than one way. If the network segment is 192.168.1, then the host identifier is 10. But if the network identifier is 192.168, then the host segment is 1.10. How is a poor router supposed to know what you want it to do?

Don't worry. There's not one but two ways to represent a subnet mask. Using the Classless Inter-Domain Routing (CIDR) notation, you would add a slash and a number after the address to tell routers what's really up. Assuming the network segment of an address takes up the first three octets (192.168.1), then the CIDR way would describe your laptop as 192.168.1.10/24 (where 24 means that the first 24 bits of this 32-bit address represent the network). If, on the other hand, you wanted only a 16-bit network segment, then you'd write it as 192.168.1.10/16—and the host segment would be 1.10.

The second approach to notation involves specifying a netmask. Using netmasks, 192.168.1.10/24 would have a netmask of 255.255.255.0, while the netmask for 192.168.1.10/16 would be 255.255.0.0.

There's a great deal of math, engineering, and perhaps even physics that'll go into architecting networks—most of which falls way beyond the scope of this book. But I will share one fundamental principle of network design. If your network segment is 192.168.1, then it stands to reason that you could have a separate network segment (also known as a *subnet*) of 192.168.2, another of 192.168.3, and so on. This kind of segmentation makes it possible to keep networks serving different functions separated. Perhaps a small business might want one network for their production infrastructure, another one for the developers, a third for the front-office staff, and a fourth for unauthenticated guests.

One more thought: you're not limited to netmask values of 255 or 0. You can designate only part of an octet for network addresses and the rest for hosts. Calculating subnets is complicated, but you can easily find online calculators that'll do the heavy work for you. If you're curious, search for *online subnet calculator*.

NAT Address Translation

The underlying concept of NAT addressing is that not all connected devices require their own unique public addresses. Sure, mobile devices that regularly move between networks will, by the nature of the way they work, need to be directly accessible from anywhere. But addressing for the PCs or servers that sit behind the router provided by your Internet service provider (ISP) could be managed at the local network level. This, in practice, has freed up countless millions of public addresses, successfully delaying the depletion of IPv4 addresses by decades.

How does it work? A single device like your ISP's Internet-facing router—working with a single public IP address—could assign *private* addresses to all the devices sitting "behind" it on the local network. Any traffic moving between those devices and the Internet would be redirected to the appropriate target by the router using address translation. Address translation, as illustrated in Figure 4.2, involves "translating" the local, private address associated with traffic coming from a local device to the public address used by the router and, on the return trip, back again to the private address.

FIGURE 4.2 A NAT server translating IP addresses and managing traffic between local and public hosts

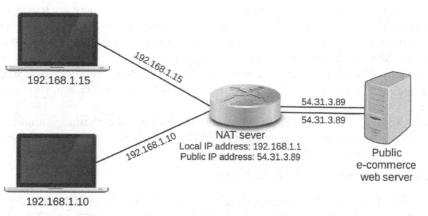

192.168.1.15

192.168.1.15

54.31.3.89

54.31.3.89

NAT sever
Local IP address: 192.168.1.1
Public IP address: 54.31.3.89

192.168.1.10

Public
e-commerce
web server

192.168.1.10

To make this work, the IP standard divides all addresses into two categories: public and private. Private addresses fall into these three ranges.

10.0.0.0 to 10.255.255.255

172.16.0.0 to 172.31.255.255

192.168.0.0 to 192.168.255.255

There are, within those ranges, more than 17 million available addresses, which should be enough for pretty much any private infrastructure environment (the devices in my house still only use up around 20 addresses—we've got quite some head room to go). Besides a very small number of special reserved addresses, all other addresses are fully routable and are available for public use. They're managed by the Internet Corporation for Assigned Names and Numbers (ICANN).

IPv6 Addressing

The second and more permanent solution to the IPv4 limit is to switch addressing from 32-bit to 128-bit. How many unique addresses can you squeeze out of a 128-bit range? I honestly don't know what you would call the number. In theory, at least, there are 2^128 possible addresses, if that helps. The point is that the standard makes it pretty much impossible to even find enough physical space in the known universe to hold enough devices to be assigned all of the available addresses. And the Wi-Fi signals needed to keep all the data moving would probably bake all life into nonexistence.

That's the good news (the expanded address range, not the bit about baking all life into nonexistence). The bad news is that IPv6 addresses are rather hard to read and even harder to remember. Instead of the four octets making up an IPv4 address, IPv6 comes with eight. And they're separated by colons rather than dots. Here's an example of a nonroutable, link-local address that was automatically assigned to a network interface on one of my machines:

```
fe80::fc9b:9cff:fee2:ffd6/64
```

I'm sure you noticed one more important difference from IPv4: there are letters, and not just numbers, in that soup. Well, technically, those are numbers, too. You see, IPv6 addresses use a hexadecimal (base 16) numbering system that uses the numbers 0–9 and then the first six letters of the English (or, more accurately, Latin) alphabet. "a" is 10, and "f" equals 15. Take another look at that address, and you should see something else that's a bit strange. Did you catch it? There are only five groups of numbers, not eight. Oh, and there are two colons in a row after the first group.

So, what's going on here? Well, the two colons actually are shorthand for multiple groups of zeros that happen to sit next to each other in the address's full version. Here's how that particular address would look in all its pristine glory:

```
fe80:0000:0000:0000:fc9b:9cff:fee2:ffd6/64
```

The final stop on our IPv6 tour is that /64 suffix. As you've probably already guessed, IPv6 addresses are divided between network and host sections in much the same way as we do it with IPv4. The only way to specify it here, however, is using the CIDR notation. The main difference, though, is that we're working with 128 bits of data rather than 32, so /64 is going to be *much* more common than something like /16.

It's worth noting that, at the network link-layer level, devices are identified by hardware or Media Access Control (MAC) addresses rather than IP addresses. MAC addresses are usually 48 bits long and are expressed as 12 hexadecimal digits. Connecting IP addresses with a specific device can be performed by routers using some form of address resolution.

Understanding the Domain Name System

The IP addresses managed by the TCP/IP protocols are the backbone of modern network administration. But you'll probably seldom directly interact with them in your daily activities. Instead, you access network resources using human-readable names like `freecodecamp.org` or `bootstrap-it.com`. But the fact is the only way your browser can understand what you're referring to with such names is by consulting a database of IP address/domain name pairs provided as part of the Domain Name System (DNS).

The particular address translation database your browser consults might spend its days in your PC's filesystem, on a stand-alone server within your network, on your Internet service provider's servers, or as a net-wide service run by companies like Google or OpenDNS. Whichever combination of DNS servers your computer is configured to consult, it begins with a request for the IP address that corresponds with, say, my `bootstrap-it.com`. You can try this yourself from the command-line terminal on any computer using the `host` command (or `nslookup` for Windows users):

```
$ host bootstrap-it.com
bootstrap-it.com has address 52.3.203.146
```

With that reply in hand, your browser will fire off a request to the web server using the 52.3.203.146 address. If everything works as planned, the contents of the default home page of my Bootstrap IT site will load in your browser.

Technically, that's known as *forward DNS* searching. But it's also sometimes necessary to translate IP addresses back to their domain name equivalents. This might be to track down the source of spam emails or other criminal activity. Such searches are, predictably known as *reverse DNS*.

Besides the fact that DNS is a critical component of all modern network activity, making sure it's properly configured is also a big deal from a security perspective. Think about what could happen if the wrong people surreptitiously responded to your DNS request for the IP of `mybank.com` where you plan to log in and pay some bills. Are you sure that the IP you got in reply is legitimate? What would happen if you were unknowingly sent to a fake bank site and fooled into entering your authentication information? Such things do happen using attack techniques like DNS spoofing or DNS hijacking.

Auditing Networks

The next step once you know how networks work is to learn how to analyze the state of the private network you're using for your devices. By "private network" here, I mean all the wired and wireless connections that exist on *your* side of the modem/router your ISP provided that connects you to the Internet. There are two main things we'll be looking for in our audit: open ports and rogue hosts.

A network port is a mechanism for routing TCP or UDP network requests to be handled by specific functions on a server. Adding port 80 to a network address, for instance, will tell the server that you're looking for a response from a Hypertext Transfer Protocol (HTTP) server, while port 22 indicates that you're in the market for opening a Secure Shell (SSH) session. Should such a service exist on the server you're connecting to—and should you satisfy any authentication requirements—you should get the response you're after.

A port is considered "open" when there's software on a server configured to listen for incoming requests and "closed" when there's no such software running. If, during a network audit, you see ports listed as open and listening that have no business being open and listening, you should take the proper steps to shut them down. It might also be a good idea to figure out why they were open in the first place.

The expression "hosts" is just a techie way of describing a PC, server, or other device when it's attached to a network. A "rogue host" is a device that's attached to your network through a switch or other connector without the knowledge or authorization of the network's owner. The kinds of trouble a host with this kind of a front-row seat to your infrastructure can get into should be deeply troubling to you. So you'll want to know what's there as soon as possible.

Uncovering unnecessarily open ports and rogue hosts will be the topic of the next sections.

Network Auditing Tools

Regularly implementing scans using an audit paradigm is, as far as I know, the only way to get useful visibility into your network. You'll want to know what's there, what's open, and, if there is something fishy going on, what exactly it's trying to accomplish. Here, we're going to look at the two cross-platform tools most closely associated with each of those tasks: Nmap and Wireshark.

Nmap (Mapping)

Installing Nmap isn't hard. And it's free. For Linux users, it'll take you nothing more than `apt install nmap` (for Debian, Ubuntu, or Mint) or `yum install nmap` (if Fedora, CentOS, or Red Hat Linux is your thing). If you're on Windows, check out this official guide on the Nmap website: `https://nmap.org/book/inst-windows.html`. And this will do it for you on macOS: `https://nmap.org/book/inst-macosx.html`.

Straightforward Nmap scans are, well, straightforward. But don't think this thing doesn't go very deep, too. The Linux version of Nmap's official user guide runs nearly 1,000 lines long. You can apply a very wide range of options to finely control the results returned by a search. And you can point Nmap to multiple hosts at once by passing it long lists of targets from text files. Output data can be redirected to external files formatted to various standards.

But here we'll stick with straightforward. Before you can actually begin scanning your network, you'll need to open a command-line shell so you can figure out the specific address subnet your network uses. On a Windows or macOS machine, that'll require running the `ipconfig` command. On modern Linux distributions, `ip a` will do the trick. Here's what a typical output on a Linux machine might look like:

```
```
$ ip a
1: lo: <LOOPBACK,UP,LOWER_UP> mtu 65536 qdisc noqueue state UNKNOWN group
default qlen 1000
```
```

```
    link/loopback 00:00:00:00:00:00 brd 00:00:00:00:00:00
    inet 127.0.0.1/8 scope host lo
       valid_lft forever preferred_lft forever
    inet6 ::1/128 scope host
       valid_lft forever preferred_lft forever
7: eth0@if8: <BROADCAST,MULTICAST,UP,LOWER_UP> mtu 1500 qdisc noqueue state UP group
default qlen 1000
    link/ether 00:16:3e:53:d4:ce brd ff:ff:ff:ff:ff:ff link-netnsid 0
    inet 10.0.3.80/24 brd 10.0.3.255 scope global dynamic eth0
       valid_lft 3224sec preferred_lft 3224sec
    inet6 fe80::216:3eff:fe53:d4ce/64 scope link
       valid_lft forever preferred_lft forever
```
```

The first entry is called lo—which stands for "loopback" and represents a virtual net
work connection to your local system. By convention, that connection's "inet" address is
127.0.0.1. The entry marked 7 that's identified as eth0 is the actual network interface, and,
as you can see on the entry's third line, its inet address is 10.0.3.80 and its IPv4 network is
configured as 24-bit. That's all I'll need to know, because it means that the network subnet
I'm on is defined as 10.0.3.0/24—I simply need to substitute 0 for whatever the host part of
the address was, which would have been 80 in my case.

Let's begin our scanning with a quick survey of TCP ports on the network. The -F option
tells Nmap to run in fast mode, which means that it will scan only 100 ports on each host it
discovers, rather than the 1,000 most common ports it would scan by default. In some cases
you might, of course, want Nmap to scan all 65,000+ ports, but that'll take much longer to
complete. Using -F here will be helpful to give us a quick sense of what hosts are present on
the network.
```
```
$ nmap -F 10.0.3.0/24

Starting Nmap 7.60 ( https://nmap.org ) at 2019-08-05 09:26 EDT
Nmap scan report for workstation (10.0.3.1)
Host is up (0.00019s latency).
Not shown: 96 closed ports
PORT     STATE SERVICE
22/tcp   open  ssh
53/tcp   open  domain
631/tcp  open  ipp

Nmap scan report for 10.0.3.80
Host is up (0.00018s latency).
```

```
All 100 scanned ports on 10.0.3.80 are closed
Nmap scan report for 10.0.3.88
Host is up (0.00020s latency).
Not shown: 98 closed ports
PORT   STATE SERVICE
22/tcp open  ssh
80/tcp open  http

Nmap scan report for 10.0.3.177
Host is up (0.00020s latency).
Not shown: 99 closed ports
PORT   STATE SERVICE
22/tcp open  ssh

Nmap done: 256 IP addresses (4 hosts up) scanned in 2.37 seconds
```

Because we told Nmap that the network was 24-bit, there were only 256 possible host addresses to look for (between 10.0.3.0 and 10.0.3.255). Among those 256 theoretical addresses, Nmap found four actual hosts. The first host—with an assigned IP of 10.0.3.1—has three ports open: 22 for SSH, 53 for DNS requests, and 631 to manage printers using the Common Unix Printing System (CUPS) admin tool. The second host (10.0.3.80) has no open ports among the 100 scanned. The other two hosts are listening for SSH requests, with one of them also acting as a web server through port 80.

With this information, your job would be to make sure you can fully account for each of the hosts and the services running on them. In other words, if you're not aware of four authorized devices matching the four Nmap found running in your network, you'll better be ready to take a careful look through the building for unnoticed cables, plugged in devices, or Wi-Fi connections.

You can also use Nmap to scan a single computer by passing just that computer's IP address (nmap 192.168.1.6) or hostname (nmap workstation.local). Using localhost instead of an IP or hostname will get Nmap to scan the machine you're currently on. This can be useful for confirming that no ports of your own computer are open without you knowing. Adding -p "*" tells Nmap to scan all ports. Finally, when you use the -O option, Nmap will try to guess what operating system the target is running. This can be particularly useful for identifying a rogue device: seeing Linux in an all-Windows shop should be of concern.

Wireshark

Wireshark is a network packet analyzer. Why would you ever want to analyze network packets? Because, as you've already seen, network packets contain loads of interesting information about who's connected and communicating with machines in your network, what kinds of software are involved, and, to some degree, what those packets actually contain.

Here's one scenario. Suppose, using Nmap, you did discover an unexpected device on your network but couldn't immediately figure out what it was and what it was there for. Make sure you've already installed Wireshark (consult www.wireshark.org/download .html) and then go ahead and fire it up. From the list that appears on the intro screen, double-click the interface that's connected to the network you're working with. Because there's a lot happening on this particular workstation, the intro screen shown in Figure 4.3 may seem bewildering. But yours will probably have only two or three choices.

FIGURE 4.3   The Wireshark "home" screen showing links to all the networks available to the system

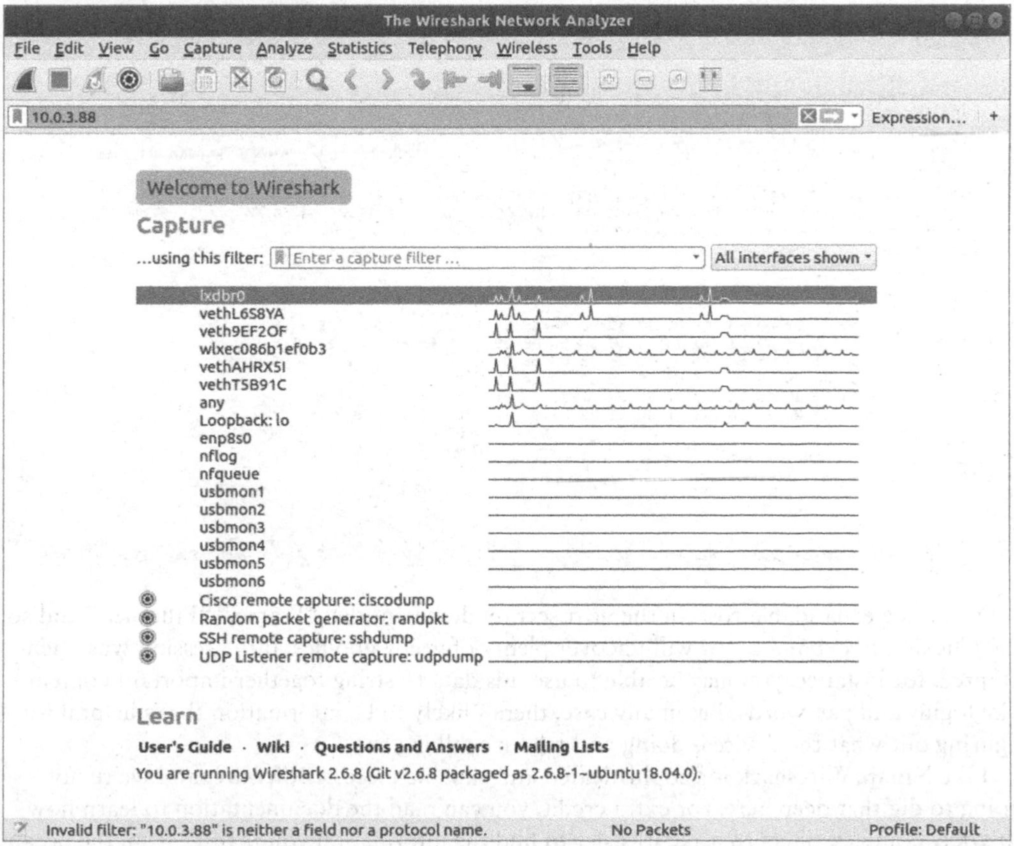

The capture view (shown in Figure 4.4) includes a filter bar near the top. In the figure, I've already entered the 10.0.3.88 IP address of the suspicious device and started the capture. Each of the numbered rows just below (numbered 4, 5, 6, etc.,) represents a single packet and displays the packet source (the IP address 8.8.8.8 in the case of row 4), its destination (the machine we're watching: 10.0.3.88), the protocol it's using (ICMP), and the kind of message the packet carried. This one was a reply to a ping request, sent to confirm that the Google DNS server (8.8.8.8) was listening.

FIGURE 4.4   The results of a typical network scan shown in Wireshark

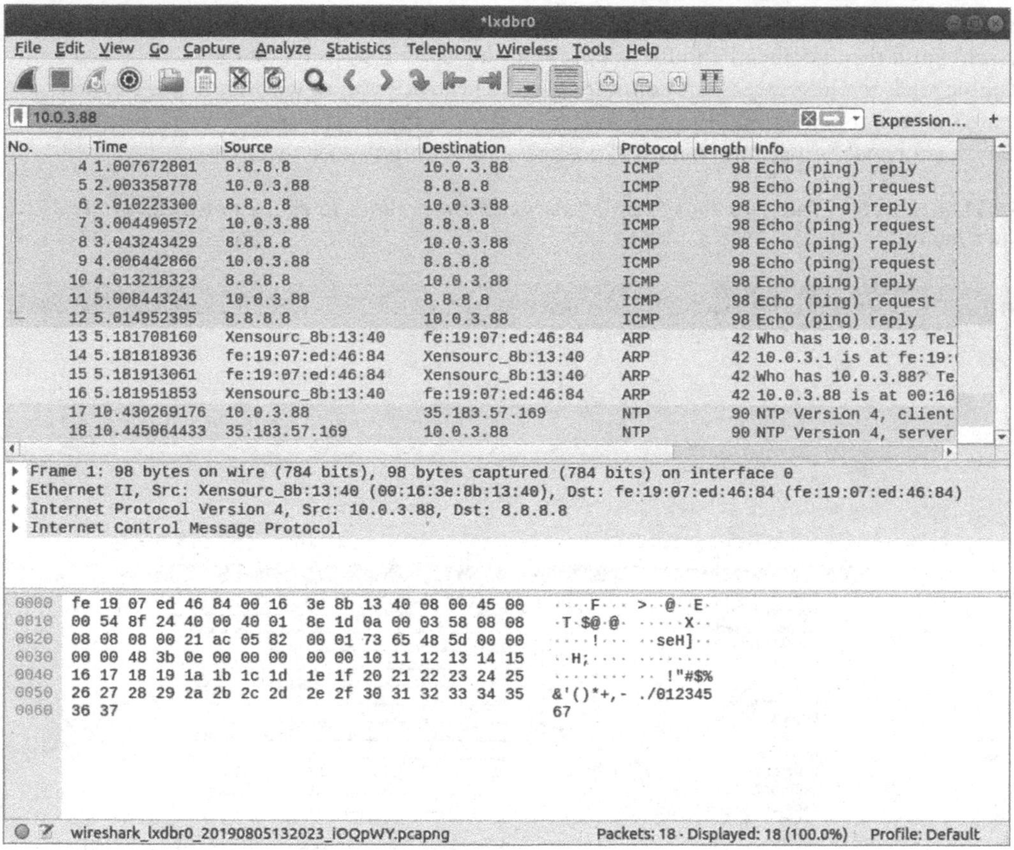

You'll see expandable rows in the next section down entitled "Frame," "Ethernet," and so on. Clicking to expand a row will uncover plenty of geeky goodies. If the session was unencrypted, for instance, you may be able to use this data to string together important content—like logins and passwords. But in any case, there's likely to be information that's helpful for figuring out what the device is doing and who it's talking to.

Like Nmap, Wireshark is a sophisticated and capable piece of software, and we're not going to dig that deep here. For extra credit, you can read the documentation to learn how to apply complex filters to make it easier to find the information you're after from the ocean of data that Wireshark delivers. You can also learn how to write Wireshark (or Nmap) output to PCAP-formatted files so it can be archived and analyzed in an environment that's a better fit for your needs.

Automating Audits

Knowing how to scan and assess your network assets is great, but it won't do you a lot of good if you don't apply your skills both early and often. In high-risk or high-value environments, you should be running a serious scan at least once a week. But you know that this is just the sort of task that you're not likely to remember to perform more after the first little while, right? So let me introduce you to the admin's best friend: automation.

The specific details might vary from one OS to the next, but the general approach is the same: anything worth doing on a computer can be converted to a script and then set to run on its own on a schedule. Nmap even comes with more than 500 prebuilt scripts for performing tasks like testing a WordPress installation for weak passwords (`http-wordpress-brute.nse`) or a web server for weak encryption configurations (`ssl-enum-ciphers.nse`). On a Linux machine with Nmap installed, you'll find those scripts in the `/usr/share/nmap/scripts/` directory.

How about Wireshark? Is there a way to automate the operations of a GUI application? In a word: yes. But it'll require you to install the TShark command-line version of Wireshark. Using TShark, you can run complex scans involving all the filtering goodness you love so much about Wireshark and incorporate them within your own custom scripts. And just like Wireshark, you can write your output to a PCAP file.

Just as an example, this little gem of a command will have TShark watch DNS address requests and output a list of all the domain names that are requested over the duration of the scan:

```
tshark -i eth0 -f "dst port 53" -n -T fields -e dns.qry.name
```

`-i` points to the device's network interface (eth0 on this Linux machine). `-f` will filter the captured data to retrieve only packets sent to TCP or UDP port 53 (the DNS port). `-n` will disable network object name resolution. `-T fields` allows the output format to be set to `dns.qry.name` as specified by the value of `-e`.

Of course, that's only half the battle. Someone's going to have to read the results before all those scans add any value to the equation. The simplest way to do that is to automate the data that's produced by your scans, filter out all but the most pressing results, and have a digest of those pushed to the admins responsible for the system. Doesn't sound simple enough for you? Then perhaps you should hang around until Chapter 7, "Risk Assessment," where we'll learn about some of the tools available for performing comprehensive vulnerability scans.

Securing Networks

The right responses to the problems surfaced by the auditing tools we've discussed in this chapter will usually be pretty obvious. If it's not supposed to be there, remove it. If it's configured wrong, fix it. But you should also give thought to some proactive actions that, if incorporated into your IT operations, can go a long way toward *preventing* trouble. That's what we'll explore through the rest of this chapter.

Patch Your Software

There's no way to overstate this. Considering how complex and chaotic software development can be, you should expect that bugs will be discovered and new threat models introduced. Even if you were careful when choosing and then installing software packages on your system, there's no guarantee their integrity will persist indefinitely. As new threats appear, actively managed software should be fairly quickly patched, with updates made publicly available. Historically, Linux developers have been better at providing timely patches, but all responsible software vendors are doing their best.

The first thing to consider, however, is whether the providers of the software you're using are responsible or if those projects are actively managed at all. Companies go out of business, and the people standing behind open-source projects move on to other challenges, or even become ill or die. It's your responsibility to keep an eye on the status of your system resources. How's that done?

- Spend a little time each day scanning the technology news headlines for developments that can impact your systems. In one form or another I've been keeping up with the industry using ZDNet (www.zdnet.com) for 30 years, now. But there are lots of websites, email newsletters, and social media resources out there to fit your needs and interests. To illustrate what I mean, just an hour before writing these words, my daily ZDNet email alerted me to a newly discovered unpatched vulnerability directly threatening some of the systems I manage. You must keep your eyes and ears open.

- If your OS provides an automated update feature, enable it. I realize that updates have caused serious usability issues for Windows users in particular in the past—which was one of the main reasons I personally switched to Linux many years ago—but the risks of ignoring security updates are huge. At the least, think carefully about your options and try to find a solution that balances security against your productivity needs.

And remember that software updates are important for all your devices, not just PCs and servers. Network routers and smartphones run on software that's just as likely to require updates as any other. The only difference is that you're not as likely to think about those devices when the topic of updates comes up, and the update process is usually not nearly as simple.

Physically Secure Your Infrastructure

Do you personally know the identities of everyone who comes through your building on a given day? Are there network switches or even live Ethernet connections sitting unprotected in publicly accessible spaces? Are you sharing office space with other organizations whose members include people you don't recognize? How easy would it be for someone claiming to be there to deliver a package or to fill in for your regular cleaning crew to quietly slip a malicious USB flash drive into the back of a PC or to leave a tiny, single-board computer designed to sniff network local traffic and send results back home (IBM researchers have already demonstrated how easy this can be)?

Spend some time taking a good look around your facility and think about all the terrible ways your current setup could be abused. And then take some time to fill in all the holes. Most of all, create a practical set of security policies so that, moving forward, you can be confident that when the next disaster hits, at least it won't be your fault.

Secure Your Network Behavior

Even once you've addressed your physical and infrastructure vulnerabilities, there will still be plenty of openings for attack. But a lot of those risks can be reduced by the way you think and behave around your technology. Part of the game might involve adjusting the expectations you hold for your IT investments. And another part will require you to think about simple patterns of behavior that could innocently be exposing you to unnecessary risk.

Consider wireless connectivity. Accessing resources through your smartphone's data service, from a security perspective, isn't all that different than the ADSL or cable connection you use at home. But connecting through Wi-Fi access points can spell trouble—especially if they're connections using no or very weak encryption. Are you sure the Wi-Fi network you're connecting to in a public place is safe? The problem is that we often expect to be able to consume digital data wherever we happen to be, whenever we need it. The need for data can be so strong that when a safe connection is unavailable, many of us will—"just this one time, really!"—rely on whatever's available.

Similarly, you surely know that bright, flashing websites offering free downloads of movies or software are dangerous. I mean, it doesn't make sense that a Hollywood studio would spend a hundred million dollars making a product only to happily give it away. And how likely is it that the owners of the download site wouldn't be just as comfortable stealing something from your computer the same way they took that movie? Suspicious downloads are suspicious for a reason. Don't be the one who opens the door to the malware that wipes out your IT assets.

If you *do* decide to take a chance, at least calculate the possible consequences. High-value targets like your online banking account, for instance, should be exposed to only minimal risk. That could mean resolving to never access your bank through a public Wi-Fi network—or perhaps only from your home PC. It's all about balancing risk against need.

Securing Your Wireless Connections

Make sure you always connect to Wi-Fi networks (whether public or private) through routers that are configured to insist on securely encrypted and password-protected client logins. The current state of the art for Wi-Fi encryption is the WPA2 standard (rather than the badly outdated WEP or WPA standards), but keep your eyes open for new protocols that prove better at protecting your connections, like the recently announced WPA3.

When you provide your own local Wi-Fi access, keep in mind that you're effectively inviting participants into your local private network. This gives them access to what's known as the network link layer. Link-layer access in general is often an important part of the administration, monitoring, and analysis of network operations. But it does open up the potential for risk. You should therefore ensure that the individual devices on your local network are appropriately secured.

Other Stuff

You never really finish the job of tightening up your network security: there are just too many possible details and, anyway, the rules keep changing. You can never afford to completely turn your attention away from the problem. Some important tasks will be addressed later in the book, including encrypting your connections and, where appropriate, using virtual private networks (VPNs) for communication. You'll also learn about designing infrastructure architecture with resource isolation in mind. But, to wrap up this chapter, I'll just throw a few more loosely connected ideas your way.

Be aware of some common classes of networking devices. While the precise purpose and function of these devices can sometimes overlap, they do have individual definitions.

- A switch is a device containing multiple Ethernet network ports through which computers and other devices can connect to each other, forming a network.

- A router is a device that coordinates and controls the movement of data packets across one or more networks and between connected devices. A *default router* (or *gateway*) is the network node that serves to forward data between a local and remote networks.

- An access point is a bridge between wired and wireless networks that connects wireless devices to each other, to a wired router, and to the Internet beyond.

When you perform a network audit the way we described earlier, give some special thought to any connected devices you find. A network printer, a file sharing device, or even a smart fridge might be advertising its own network services to anyone passing through the neighborhood. By default, some of those devices are set to provide passwordless access and, once someone's in, it's hard to know how far that access can extend beyond the device itself. The bottom line is that anything you own that comes with wireless capabilities should be locked down and available to only authorized users.

Finally, be especially paranoid about your email accounts—especially the ones you use for authenticating into other services. A single email address that's used as a login ID for multiple online services becomes a single point of attack should it be compromised. To illustrate, if your Gmail account credentials are ever compromised and, as a result, your identity is stolen, the thief might then be able to reset the passwords you used with that address for other services as though it was you. For such accounts, try to use excellent passwords and multifactor authentication (MFA) the way you saw in Chapter 3, "Controlling Access to Your Assets." It can also be a good idea to limit the number of accounts associated with any one email address.

Summary

TCP/IP refers to a suite of standards and protocols that govern network connections (TCP) and host addressing (IP).

Understanding the structure and function of IPv4 and IPv6 addressing is critical to grasping nearly all network security processes.

Smart network segmentation allows efficient and secure administration of larger IT infrastructure stacks.

Domain Name System (DNS) databases translate requests for human-friendly network addresses (like `bootstrap-it.com`) into machine-friendly IP addresses. Without a working DNS server, most normal Internet activity would be impossible.

Network scanning and packet analysis can be performed using tools like Nmap and Wireshark. You can use such tools to look for unauthorized or other dangerous activity on your network.

It's critical to automate regular network scans—including vulnerability reporting protocols—so you always remain aware of the state and status of your network resources.

Regularly patching your OSs and software, keeping up with IT developments, protecting your physical infrastructure, and maintaining discipline in the way you use your networks are all important elements of an effective network security regimen.

Exam Essentials

Understand the differences between IPv4 and IPv6 addresses.   IPv4 addresses are made up of four 8-bit octets, each a number between 0 and 256. IPv6 addresses contain eight hexadecimal octets and, using 128-bit address spaces, provide the potential for practically unlimited host addresses.

Understand how Network Address Translation (NAT) address management works.   A NAT router converts private IP addresses to a single public IP address whenever packets are sent between the Internet and a local host.

Understand how netmasks identify the network and host values of an IP address.   Both IPv4 and IPv6 addresses are made up of network and host identifiers. The network section (to the left) defines the identity of the controlling network while the segments to the right identify a specific host device. Either CIDR or dotted-decimal notations are used to define which segments belong to the network as opposed to the host sections.

Understand the basic function of network ports.   A network port is a way to communicate to the server listening on a particular IP address which service you're interested in accessing. Common TCP port numbers include 22 for SSH and 80 for unencrypted HTTP websites. An "open" port represents software that's running and listening for external client requests.

Understand the basic functions of the Nmap network scanning tool.   Nmap will scan a network—or an individual host—for running devices and, within devices, for listening services (i.e., open ports).

Understand the basic functions of the Wireshark packet analysis tool.   Wireshark can deconstruct and display the data and metadata of data packets as they move through your network.

Review Questions

1. What best describes the Transmission Control Protocol (TCP)?
   A. The protocol defining how remote connections can be securely encrypted
   B. The protocol defining how applications at either end of a connection communicate with each other
   C. The protocol defining how network packets are directed between source and destination hosts
   D. The protocol defining a bidirectional interactive text-oriented communication facility

2. What is the primary purpose of an IP address?
   A. To allow delivery of data to a host on a network
   B. To allow administrators to track all operations to their owners
   C. To allow reliable identification of a network subnet range
   D. To increase network efficiency

3. Which of the following are valid IPv4 IP addresses? (Choose two.)
   A. 10.0.260.10
   B. 192.168.1.34
   C. 54.99.0.101
   D. 22.198.65/24

4. Approximately how many possible IP addresses are, in theory at least, available through the IPv4 protocol?
   A. 4,000,000,000,000
   B. 1024^16
   C. 256
   D. 4,000,000,000

5. Which of the four octets of the 192.168.4.0/24 address represent the network?
   A. 192.168.4
   B. 168.4.0
   C. /24
   D. 192.168

6. What is the principal benefit of using NAT network configurations for IPv4 networking?
   A. By using NAT addressing, you can better limit the misuse of addressing through scams like address spoofing.
   B. NAT network simplifies network configuration administration.
   C. NAT networking permits faster and more efficient data transfers.
   D. By restricting all local, private hosts to the three RFC 1918 private address ranges, you free up many millions of addresses for public devices.

7. Which of the following best describes an IPv6 address?
   A. Eight 16-bit octets made up of hexadecimal numbers
   B. Sixteen 16-bit octets made up of hexadecimal numbers
   C. Sixteen 16-bit octets made up of numbers between 0–9
   D. Four 8-bit octets made up of hexadecimal numbers

8. Which of the following are valid IPv6 addresses? (Choose two.)
   A. fe80:0000:0000:0000:9cff:fee2:ffd6/64
   B. fe80::fc9b:9cff:fee2:ffd6/64
   C. fe80:::fc9b:9cff:fee2:ffd6/64
   D. fe80:0000:0000:0000:fc9b:9cff:fee2:ffd6/64

9. What is the primary purpose of the Domain Name System (DNS)?
   A. To control the distribution of blocks of IP addresses
   B. To translate numeric IP addresses into human-readable URLs
   C. To translate human-readable URLs into numeric IP addresses
   D. To ensure no two websites are trying to use the same address

10. Which of the following is used to define the network portion of an IP address?
    A. Netmask
    B. Subnet
    C. Domain
    D. Host

11. Which of the following IP addresses are, by convention, permitted for use in private NAT networks? (Choose two.)
    A. 192.168.9.200
    B. 10.0.5.48
    C. 196.168.9.200
    D. 28.120.16.32

12. What information does a typical security audit of your network look for? (Choose two.)
    A. Unauthorized devices connected to your network
    B. Poorly formed network addresses
    C. Unnecessarily open listening ports
    D. Insufficient routing hardware to keep up with network loads

13. Which of the following Nmap commands will search only the 100 most commonly open TCP ports on the 10.0.4.0/24 network?
    A. `nmap -p 10.0.4.0`
    B. `nmap -F 10.0.4.0/24`
    C. `nmap 10.0.4.0/24`
    D. `nmap -f 10.0.4.0/24`

14. Which of the following data types are included in a typical Wireshark output? (Choose three.)

    A. Packet size

    B. Packet process ID

    C. Packet protocol

    D. Packet destination

15. What tool makes it possible to create automated scripts of the kinds of complex filtered scans that the GUI Wireshark would normally perform?

    A. `wiresharkd`

    B. `tshark`

    C. `Nmap`

    D. `wired`

16. From a security perspective, what should you look for before downloading and installing software? (Choose two.)

    A. Software made by developers who meet execution deadlines and remain within budget

    B. Software made by developers who regularly maintain and patch their product

    C. Software made by developers whose companies are active and have solid reputations

    D. Software made by developers who are known to produce software with few or no bugs

17. Which of the following should you do to physically secure your servers and other compute devices? (Choose three.)

    A. Define procedures to control who has access to the buildings and key locations used to maintain your organization's infrastructure.

    B. Regularly scan your network for unauthorized devices.

    C. Enforce rules governing the use of password and biometric authentication.

    D. Restrict the use of webcams and other video devices to only when absolutely necessary.

18. Within the context of network security, which of the following are the most important ideas you should be teaching the members of your organization? (Choose two.)

    A. Configure your wireless networks to permit only authorized use.

    B. Carefully monitor your facility's power supply.

    C. Never let people you don't know into the facility.

    D. Avoid visiting suspicious, high-risk websites.

19. Which of the following devices present the greatest threats to your network? (Choose two.)

    A. Old and outdated PCs

    B. Wi-Fi devices configured to use poor or no encryption

    C. Improperly configured Internet of Things devices

    D. CAT5 or older Ethernet cabling

20. From the perspective of network security, what advantages are Linux distributions more likely to have over other operating systems?

   A. The Linux kernel protects against incursions by default.

   B. Open-source software will, by definition, almost never contain malware.

   C. Viruses cannot infect Linux systems.

   D. Most, if not all, of the software you use will come from curated repositories.

Chapter 5

Encrypting Your Data at Rest

THE LPI SECURITY ESSENTIALS EXAM
TOPICS COVERED IN THIS CHAPTER
INCLUDE THE FOLLOWING:

✓ **022.1 Cryptography and public key infrastructure**

- Understanding of the concepts of symmetric, asymmetric, and hybrid cryptography

- Understanding of the concepts of hash functions, ciphers, and key exchange algorithms

- Understanding of the concepts of Public Key Infrastructures (PKI), Certificate Authorities, and Trusted Root-CAs

- Awareness of important cryptographic algorithms

✓ **022.4 Data storage encryption**

- Understanding of the concepts of data, file, and storage device encryption

- Using VeraCrypt to store data in an encrypted container or an encrypted storage device

- Understanding the core features of BitLocker

- Using Cryptomator to encrypt files stored in file storage cloud services

It may not be obvious to people without a lot of experience with IT operations, but, unless you actively intervene, most of the data you produce and consume using your compute devices can be easily copied and read by just about anyone. That includes the spreadsheets you attach to emails to your boss, the images and videos you move around on a USB flash drive, and even the thousands of work files you've got on your laptop.

The general rule is that if, in its default state, you can read your data, so can anyone else. As long as no one else has access to your storage drives, that's not a problem. But if you're planning to move data across a network—or if there's a chance that, say, your laptop could be stolen or compromised by hackers—then you'd better find a way to protect yourself.

The protection of choice for digital data is one form or another of encryption. In this chapter, you'll learn how encryption works, how it's commonly applied in the real world, and how it's used as part of blockchain infrastructure (and just what a *blockchain* is). I'll also introduce you to some widely used and effective encryption technologies to point you toward practical next steps.

Ready? 90a11dc39f14365f6a7221eb1b5948ac.

(You'll understand what that last bit was all about a bit later.)

What Is Encryption?

The core principle behind encryption is simple and, in fact, has been in use for thousands of years. It works by applying a mathematical operation (known as an *algorithm*) to some text, which converts it to something unreadable. A very simple substitution cipher, which can work by shifting each letter by a set number of alphabet positions would, if the agreed shift was two positions to the right, transform "Hello" to "Jgnnq." As long as the legitimate recipient of the message knows that the original can be recovered by shifting two positions back, you can safely send the message through "enemy lines" since you and your recipient are the only folks around with the decryption key.

If the basics are straightforward, the problem of making them work in a world dominated by ever more powerful computers has occupied some of the world's greatest mathematical minds for the past hundred years. Some of the earliest computers were, like Alan Turning's Colossus at Bletchley Park, created specifically to decrypt secret enemy transmissions.

I strongly suspect that my childish substitution cipher wouldn't have stood much of a chance against Colossus! Modern encryption algorithms create vastly more complex results and, when used properly, will produce encrypted text that's effectively useless to anyone besides the intended recipient.

When it comes to data encryption, there are three general approaches: symmetric, asymmetric, and a hybrid of the two. Symmetric encryption requires a secret (or private) key to be present at both the encryption and decryption steps. As you can see in Figure 5.1, you might own a data file—like a spreadsheet—that you want to send securely to a small group of colleagues. At your end, you would use software to create a secret key whose contents would be invoked in converting each character of the spreadsheet file to something else. If you were to display the encrypted version of your spreadsheet, it would consist of unreadable gibberish. You can safely transmit the encrypted file over an insecure network, confident that no one can make any use of it. However, before your colleagues can decrypt it, they'll need to have an exact copy of your secret key, which they can invoke using their own software to re-convert the file to a readable spreadsheet.

FIGURE 5.1   A typical symmetric encryption and decryption process

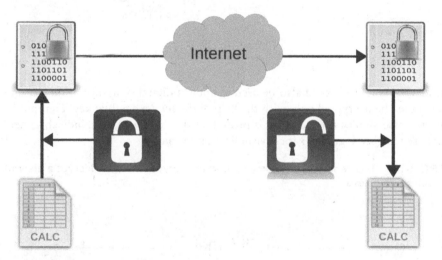

That's the major weakness of symmetric encryption: having to send a file containing the secret key back and forth in a way that protects its integrity is complicated. Eventually, someone's bound to slip up and send it as part of an unencrypted email message or leave it around on a USB flash drive that gets stolen. Once a single copy of the key is out of trusted hands, every single document it was used to encrypt is now vulnerable.

Asymmetric encryption doesn't need shared common secrets and all the trouble they cause. Instead each participant will have their own unique private key that's generated by an encryption software framework (like OpenSSH) and remains permanently and safely on that user's computer. At the same time, the encryption software will also generate a mathematically related public key that can be safely shared with participants in connections. In one variation, as shown in Figure 5.2, the original document is encrypted using the *recipient's* public key, which, being a public key, can be transferred without risk. Decryption, which takes place on the recipient's computer, can proceed only with the help of the recipient's private key.

FIGURE 5.2   The *recipient's* public key is used to encrypt and later decrypt a file with the use of both private keys.

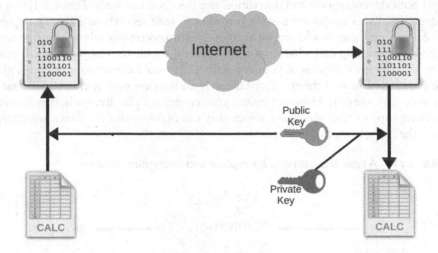

A sender's private key could also be used to apply a digital signature to the document, which can then be decrypted only with the help of the *sender's* public key. That public key, now in the possession of the recipient, is proof that the document was, indeed, signed by the legitimate sender. See Figure 5.3 for a visualization of that.

FIGURE 5.3   The *sender's* public key is used to encrypt and later decrypt a file with the use of both private keys.

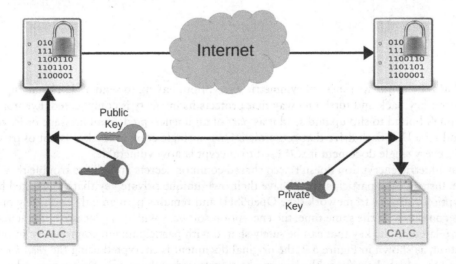

Like symmetric encryption, its asymmetric cousin has its own downside: the intensity of computation necessary to apply the needed algorithms to large amounts of moving data can slow down the exchange. To permit more efficient secure operations, most modern connection systems will use a mix—or hybrid—of symmetric and asymmetric tools. The initial key exchange will take place using a full asymmetric connection, while subsequent data will be transferred using that original key using the less compute-intensive symmetric encryption.

In any case, all this usually happens invisibly, managed automatically by the software you choose. What that software is relying on, however, is known as a *public key infrastructure* (PKI) through which public keys are bound to a particular identity. Those keys can be trusted when validated by the root certificate of a trusted *certificate authority* (CA).

Encryption Usage Patterns

Encrypting data as it's being sent between remote computers is going to be the subject of the next chapter. Here's where we're going to mostly focus on applying the principles of encryption to the task of securing data at rest. We'll also explore hashing, an alternative to encryption, and take a quick look at the encryption-heavy topic of blockchains.

What Should You Encrypt?

You've got some tough choices to make. You'll need to balance convenience against security and one potential risk against another. On the one hand, working with encrypted data drives can limit the scope of what you can do with them. Recovering data from a nonbooting drive that's encrypted, for instance, will sometimes be impossible and will certainly be more difficult. But, on the other hand, the costs associated with the theft of your unencrypted data can be significantly higher. Here are some scenarios that make particularly strong candidates for encryption:

- Devices, like laptops or smartphones, that are at high risk of theft or loss.
- Devices that are likely to contain sensitive data. A smartphone that isn't used for banking and isn't logged into a high-use online account might be one example of low risk. The general rule: if losing it would be annoying, don't bother encrypting. If losing it would be a *catastrophe*, encrypt.
- Filesystems within a larger drive containing sensitive data. If your drive is divided into multiple disk partitions, you'll probably need to encrypt only the specific partitions where key data will live. Leaving the OS and, perhaps, logs unencrypted can at least expand your options in the event of a failure.

The bottom line is that you should understand your system, your needs, and the risks you face well enough that you can encrypt only what's necessary: no more and no less.

Understanding Hashing vs. Encryption

If you want to define encryption as "obscuring data so it can't be read by the wrong people," then it's not unreasonable to expand your understanding of the field to include hashing. But there are important differences. First, though, just what is hashing?

A cryptographic hash function is a tool for mapping a message (or any string of digital data) to a string of characters of a set size. Trying to visualize what that might mean in the real world? Remember that strange hexadecimal text (90a11dc39f14365f6a7221eb1b5 948ac) I included in the chapter introduction? That was the hash created from the words "Let's get started" using the MD5 function. On my Linux machine, this is the command I used to produce it:

```
echo -n "Let's get started" | md5sum
```

Could you have deciphered that string to figure out the simple message? It's highly unlikely. So if I wanted to store my message in a format that keeps you from guessing the meaning, that would be a good choice. However, I should note that, technically speaking, the MD5 function itself is no longer considered secure: its algorithm can now be broken by commonly available computers. SHA-256 is currently a more acceptable standard.

Since we're talking about encryption algorithms, it's worth briefly describing some of the key players in the field.

- Since Advanced Encryption Standard (AES) is supported at the hardware level by most CPUs, its operations will generally be very fast. And since it's used by both SSH and TrueCrypt, you're probably using AES already.

- The RSA algorithm isn't nearly as fast as AES, but it's optimized for asymmetric encryption involving sharing secret keys and signing hashes.

- Elliptic Curve DSA (ECDSA) is based on the Elliptic Curve Discrete Logarithm Problem (ECDLP) and is considered a tough algorithm to break—something that should remain true for at least the near future. Some cryptocurrencies make use of the ECDLP in their processes. Effective ECDLP encryption does require a good source of random numbers.

- The Diffie–Hellman key exchange isn't used for encryption or signing directly, but for securely coordinating the choice of a key that's shared between two parties who want to engage in a secure exchange.

There are, as I mentioned, differences between hashes and encryption. For instance, hashing works in only one direction. That is, you can create a hash out of data, but you can't retrieve the source data from the hash. This means you can't just use hashing to obscure data in a way that can be retrieved by a remote recipient.

So, where *can* you use hashing? A hash is a great tool for storing authentication information like passwords. When you create an account and password for an online service, it would be a poor practice if the actual password would ever be visible to the service's administrators. That's why—ideally—customer support techs can't tell you what your forgotten password was.

Instead, the online software creates a hash of your password and stores it in the system. The next time you log in, the system will create a new hash of the password you enter and compare it to the one they made from the original. If they match, you're in.

One possible limitation of hashes is that a particular input text will always generate the same hash. So, if someone had access to a *rainbow table*—which contains known hashes along with their source strings—your password could be guessed using nothing more than its hash. To help prevent such abuses, a password might be *salted* before it's hashed. Salting simply adds a random character string to the input text before hashing. Without the original salt, rainbow tables won't be useful.

What Are Blockchains?

A blockchain is, as the name suggests, a chain of data blocks that can be used as a record of transactions and, later, to document and confirm their authenticity. The idea is to provide a similar function to what you'd get from an accounting ledger, but with an ongoing audit in the form of a distributed consensus.

Here's how it works. A transaction generates a data block that includes a cryptographic hash based on the transaction details. A second computer on the blockchain network will read the full contents of the first block, calculate a new hash based of that content, and create a new block that includes that hash. Subsequent members of the network will add further blocks based on the block that precedes them. Figure 5.4 is a visualization of that process.

FIGURE 5.4　The step-by-step representation of a blockchain transaction

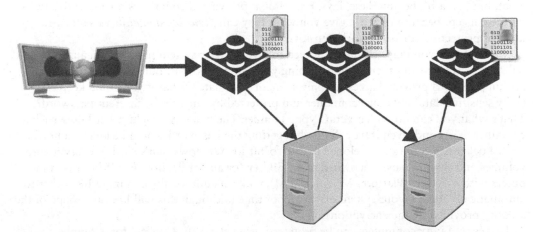

What this chain of hashes gives us is, effectively, an unbreakable verification. Should someone later try to alter the details of a transaction—perhaps to claim that he paid for a million dollars' worth of a commodity rather than just a half a million—the hash of the original block would be significantly changed. This would cause the entire chain to fail, as the hashes of each of the subsequent blocks would no longer work.

Blockchains were originally conceived as a way of reliably managing the first crypto currency: Bitcoin. Since then, it's been proposed for use in verifying a growing range of financial and institutional transactions executed over distributed networks.

From a security perspective, blockchain technologies can enhance the reliability, privacy, and security of legitimate interactions. By that same token, however, they're just as effective at providing privacy and anonymity to criminal organizations. I guess that's just how technology works.

Encryption Technologies

I'll admit that everything we've seen so far in this chapter has been a bit abstract. But now that you understand how encryption and cryptographic hashes work, it's time to take a look at some practical tools that you can use to beef up your own security.

First up: VeraCrypt, a free utility for encrypting data on storage drives. Besides the fact that it's free, there's a lot to like about VeraCrypt. It's available for Windows, macOS, and Linux, for one thing. It can be used to encrypt entire drives, individual partitions, or individual filesystems for another. But the fact that it can embed a filesystem as a virtual archive within a single file makes it interesting.

Container virtualization is hardly new in the compute world. The idea that you can convince a few directories worth of files that they're really all alone on their own physical computer and can use its hardware to to launch and run a virtual operating system session is great, but just a bit boring these days. But VeraCrypt's virtual containers are a creative twist on the concept because they can give you what they call *plausible deniability* as an extra layer of protection for particularly sensitive data.

Worried that you may one day be forced to give up your system password against your will? Force is force and there's often nothing you can do about it. But suppose your main system password provided access to only *some* of your data? What if you could keep especially sensitive data in its own container and protected by an entirely different password? That's what you can do with a VeraCrypt container. The bad guys might never know such a container exists and, even if they did find it, getting the password would be an extra hurdle.

BitLocker is a program developed by Microsoft for Windows that's used to encrypt entire volumes and require a user password or a USB key for authentication. For Windows computers with a Trusted Platform Module (TPM), you can additionally configure BitLocker to automatically unlock your system drive at boot time (although this will limit the scope of the security provided by the encryption).

Drives on Linux computers can be protected using eCryptfs. Ubuntu, for example, gives you the option of encrypting your new drive using eCryptfs during the installation process. Encrypting existing drives at any point in their life cycle is also available. eCryptfs is particularly flexible in that it lets you encrypt individual files or all the files associated with individual user accounts rather than entire drives. This can be particularly useful for scenarios where a computer—like a web server, for example—is going to be accessed by different *classes* of users.

> If you do pick and choose individual directory trees within a larger system to encrypt, make sure you don't leave anything out that should be picked and chosen. With that in mind, remember to get eCryptfs to encrypt any active swap partitions (using the `ecry-hptfs-setup-swap` command) because they will often contain plain-text versions of files from your encrypted filesystems.

`cryptsetup` is a command-line interface for the Linux kernel-based dm-crypt disk encryption system. You apply `cryptsetup` to a clean, freshly formatted drive. `cryptsetup` is particularly well suited to encrypting movable data drives—like USB flash devices. An encrypted drive can be mounted and edited on any host machine that has the software installed. The kind of scenario where this will work well might be where you need to safely carry data along while traveling. Since you'll be working on servers where you're going, you don't want to take your own laptop. Preparing an external hard drive or a USB flash drive and then saving and encrypting your data to it is a safe and simple option.

One more piece of the encryption-at-rest puzzle is the problem of cloud storage. Public cloud compute platforms like Amazon Web Services (AWS) and Microsoft Azure—along with storage-only services like Dropbox and Google Drive—are affordable and efficient tools for managing data that's highly available, but they, too, require security planning.

The AWS Key Management Service (KMS), as an example, lets you administrate the use of strong encryption keys for your data you store on, say, their Simple Storage Service (S3). You can even extend the use of KMS keys to local resources before they're uploaded to S3.

The open-source Cryptomator software offers client-side encryption for cloud files. In normal English, that means files you access locally can exist encrypted on a cloud platform and are constantly synchronized behind the scenes without your active involvement. The software works by creating what the Cryptomator people call a *vault* that lives within your account space on a cloud provider like Dropbox or Google Drive. It then creates a virtual hard drive on your local machine through which you can access and edit your files as though they were actually saved locally.

Summary

The best way to definitively protect data from unauthorized access is by obscuring it using encryption—rendering it unreadable without access to decryption keys.

Acceptable encryption standards must continually improve to keep ahead of more powerful compute technologies and their brute-force encryption key–guessing abilities.

The kind of encryption you choose will depend on the way you'll be using your data—including the level of risk to which it will be exposed.

Sensitive authentication information can be stored on servers using hashes, but those would be inappropriate for data that must be retrieved. For those, symmetric or asymmetric encryption would work better.

Hashes are used as a central element of blockchains.

Exam Essentials

Understand the basic workings of symmetric, asymmetric, and hybrid encryption tools.   Symmetric encryption involves a shared secret that both the data's sender and recipient must have. Asymmetric encryption works through a combination of private and public keys, removing the need to ever share the private key. Hybrid encryption will combine both symmetric and asymmetric schemes in a single transaction to balance security with efficiency.

Know what needs encrypting.   Assess the risks facing your data, your accessibility needs, and any ways individual filesystems can be separated from entire drives.

Understand the difference between encryption and cryptographic hashing.   Encryption uses a key to transform plain text into encrypted text. That key (or a subset of it) can later be used to retrieve the original text. A hash is a one-way journey: the original text can't be recovered. The value of hashes is that they can be used to store passwords to later confirm a match.

Understand the basic principles and uses for blockchains.   Blockchains are hashed records of transactions that, because of the distributed sources of their "blocks," are practically impossible to alter. Besides their reliability, they also permit a very high level of anonymity.

Be aware of the basic functions of encryption software packages.   VeraCrypt can encrypt entire drives or individual filesystems—including by creating a virtual container within a filesystem that protects a subset of directories and files. BitLocker is a full-drive encryption system specific to Windows. Encryption for Linux-based drives, individual partitions, or mobile devices can be managed using eCryptfs or `cryptsetup`. Cloud-based data stores can be encrypted using a cloud provider's system or the open-source package Cryptomator.

Review Questions

1. Which of the following describes the process of decryption?

   A. Applying the encryption key to encrypted text to restore it to a readable format

   B. Applying the encryption key to plain text to render the text unreadable

   C. Obscuring a plain-text packet as it's transferred between remote network locations

   D. Enhancing the efficiency of network transfers involving text-based applications

2. Having to manually send a copy of your single private encryption key to your recipient in advance is a feature of which class of encryption?

   A. Hybrid encryption

   B. Asymmetric encryption

   C. Duplex encryption

   D. Symmetric encryption

3. What is the greatest potential weakness of asymmetric encryption in relation to its alternatives?

   A. It requires exposing a private key through remote transfers.

   B. It is resource-intensive to maintain for extended remote sessions.

   C. The encryption algorithms used for asymmetric encryption are weak.

   D. Asymmetric encryption requires more human input.

4. Which best describes hashing?

   A. The decryption of asymmetrically encrypted data

   B. A reversible obscuring of data using a complicated algorithm

   C. An irreversible obscuring of data using a complicated algorithm

   D. A process that combines multiple encryption keys into a single digital signature

5. Despite the security benefits, why might you nevertheless not want to encrypt the hard drive of your laptop?

   A. An encrypted drive can be harder to access in the event of a software or hardware failure.

   B. Encryption will significantly slow down laptop operations.

   C. Encryption uses a lot of disk space.

   D. Encryption is complicated and requires a lot of background information to do right.

6. What are common uses for which blockchains can be particularly effective? (Select two.)

   A. To allow retail transactions to process more quickly

   B. To strengthen the reliability and security of digital transactions

   C. To enable the effective use of cryptocurrencies

   D. To strengthen the use of authentication passwords

7. What best describes the "chain" in blockchain?

   A. The fact that blockchain transactions can be easily traced back to the person who initiated it

   B. The fact that all transactions performed using a particular blockchain technology are linked to each other

   C. The fact that no single hash contained in a "block" within the blockchain can be altered without affecting the others

   D. The fact that blockchains depend on a full stack of security software

8. What feature does the Trusted Platform Module (TPM) enable on Windows computers?

   A. It allows you to encrypt large data objects stored across multiple drives.

   B. It allows you to even encrypt the data on solid-state drives (SSDs).

   C. It allows you to run Linux and macOS-based encryption software on Windows systems.

   D. It allows you to configure BitLocker to automatically unlock your system drive at boot time.

9. Which of the following software packages can be used across multiple platforms to encrypt the data on individual partitions?

   A. dm-crypt

   B. VeraCrypt

   C. BitLocker

   D. eCryptfs

10. Why should you consider encrypting any swap files you might have configured on your computer?

   A. *All* data should be encrypted if at all possible.

   B. Swap files can contain private information in clear text.

   C. Swap files are frequent sources of malware.

   D. Unencrypted swap files can slow down server performance.

Chapter 6

Encrypting Your Moving Data

THE LPI SECURITY ESSENTIALS EXAM TOPICS COVERED IN THIS CHAPTER INCLUDE THE FOLLOWING:

✓ **022.1 Cryptography and public key infrastructure**

- Understanding of the concept of Perfect Forward Secrecy
- Understanding of the differences between end-to-end encryption and transport encryption
- Understanding of the concepts of X.509 certificates
- Understanding of how X.509 certificates are requested and issued
- Awareness of certificate revocation
- Awareness of Let's Encrypt

✓ **022.2 Web encryption**

- Understanding of the major differences between plain-text protocols and transport encryption
- Understanding of the concepts of HTTPS
- Understanding of important fields in X.509 certificates for use with HTTPS
- Understanding of how X.509 certificates are associated with a specific website
- Understanding of the validity checks web browsers perform on X.509 certificates
- Determining whether or not a website is encrypted, including common browser messages

✓ **022.3 Email encryption**

- Understanding of email encryption and email signatures
- Understanding of OpenPGP

- Understanding of S/MIME

- Understanding of the role of OpenPGP key servers

- Understanding of the role of certificates for S/MIME

- Understanding of how PGP keys and S/MIME certificates are associated with an email address

- Using Mozilla Thunderbird to send and receive encrypted email using OpenPGP and S/MIME

✓ **023.2 Application security**

- Understanding of various sources for applications and ways to securely procure and install software

✓ **024.3 Network encryption and anonymity**

- Understanding of virtual private networks (VPN)

- Understanding of the concepts of end-to-end encryption

- Understanding anonymity and recognition in the Internet

- Identification due to link layer addresses and IP addresses

- Understanding of the concepts of proxy servers

✓ **025.1 Identity and authentication**

- Understanding of the security aspects of online banking and credit cards

Among the threat categories you encountered in Chapter 2 ("What Are Vulnerabilities and Threats?") were those attacks that target your data as it moves between hosts on a network. You can build your own PC or server into the digital equivalent of a medieval castle with a draw bridge, fortified gatehouse, and toxic moat, but the moment some of your data heads out through the main gate, it's all alone and vulnerable.

Unless, of course, you send it out into the world with its own armor. Right now, there's no better protection for data on the move than one or another form of encryption, which will work much the same way you saw it applied to data at rest in the previous chapter. So rather than establishing plain-text terminal connections with remote hosts using outdated tools like Telnet, you'll do it using the encrypted Secure Shell (SSH) protocol via a package like OpenSSH. And rather than transmitting images using the ancient File Transfer Protocol (FTP) or prehistoric fax technologies (which existed as "telefax" all the way back in the 1860s), you'll use an encrypted variation like the SSH File Transfer Protocol (SFTP) or a service providing secure fax transfers.

But the main focus of this chapter will be how you can encrypt the following:

- Data sent between a website and client browsers
- Email content
- Data generated by web browsing through the use of virtual private networks (VPNs)
- Software packages you download from remote repositories

Website Encryption

When you enter an Internet address—like amazon.com—into your browser, a request is sent to the server associated with that address. In response, the server will send the code, text, graphics, and metadata necessary to display web pages within your browser. Some pages contain forms where users enter their own data that is sent back to the website server. Whichever direction data may be traveling, if it's sent in plain text, it can be stolen or manipulated by anyone listening along the network.

That's a problem.

Why You Should Use Encryption

Browser connections using the insecure Hypertext Transfer Protocol (HTTP) will always use plain text, while the Hypertext Transfer Protocol *Secure* (HTTPS) version of the protocol provides encrypted connections. HTTPS connections use the Transport Layer Security (TLS) protocol. You can, where available, specify a secure connection by prefacing an address with *https* (`https://amazon.com` rather than `http://amazon.com`), but most sites will now automatically route you to an encrypted page regardless of the prefix you use. This is a battle fought by security experts that's largely been won.

> TLS was designed as the replacement for the now-deprecated—and insecure—Secure Sockets Layer (SSL) protocol. But old habits die hard: you'll often still hear tech folks referring to modern website encryption as "SSL." Of course, what they really mean is TLS.

But there are two scenarios where understanding the differences between secure from insecure sites is important. The first is when you as a *website owner* design your site architecture. Especially if you're planning a smaller, noncommercial site, you may be tempted to take the simpler path and go with HTTP. Don't do it. As we'll soon see, adding enterprise-level encryption to your site is much easier than you might think. And the possible consequences of relying on HTTP connections are significant, even for simple operations.

The second scenario is when you as a *consumer* consider interacting with a commercial website to make a purchase or process personal information. Before surrendering your credit card or health information, you *must* be sure your connection is encrypted. If "https" isn't part of the site address, some kind of lock icon doesn't appear next to the address, or your browser gives you a "certificate error" warning, then you should assume something is wrong. It could be a temporary configuration error, or it could be that the site you're on is a fake. But it's definitely not safe to continue with your session.

Before being satisfied that the site you're building is properly secured—or if you're a visitor concerned about the integrity of a third-party site—you can use an online service like the SSL Server Test (`www.ssllabs.com/ssltest`). Submitting the site address to such a service will return a report on the quality of the encryption setup looking like the page in Figure 6.1.

How Website Encryption Works

The basic idea is that your browser won't load a page that's supposed to be encrypted unless it's convinced that the server it's connecting to is reliable. How do you establish that kind of trust for a new connection? The system depends on the existence of reliable and widely accepted public certification authorities (CAs). A CA is a company or organization that issues encryption certificates to websites that can demonstrate they're legitimate. Once convinced, the CA sends its certificate to the website administrator who will then install it on the server.

FIGURE 6.1   The successful SSL report on the TLS configuration for the `bootstrap-it`
`.com` website

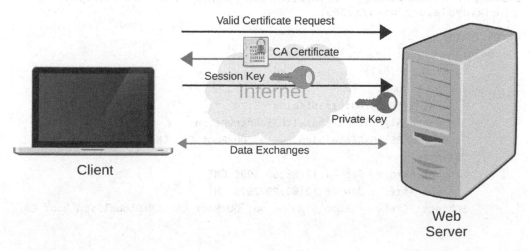

All the big-name web browsers have root certificates pre-installed by default representing the mainstream CAs. As you can see from Figure 6.2, when you point your browser to a website, the browser will ask the server whether it's got a valid certificate signed by a certificate authority and check that the key matches the CA's public key stored on the browser. Based on the server's public key, the browser will then send a new encrypted session key back to the server, which will be used for the remaining transfers of the session, with encrypted packets being decrypted as necessary at either end.

FIGURE 6.2   The conversation between a client browser and a TLS-powered web server

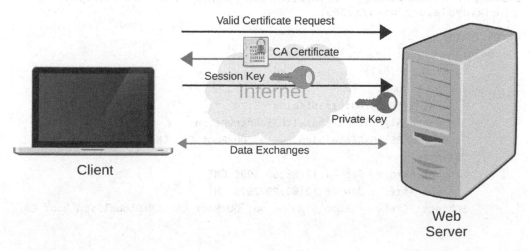

To counter the risk of session keys being compromised—endangering even data transfers from previous sessions—perfect forward secrecy (PFS) can be applied. The kind of compromise we're worried about could involve the exposure of the server's private key. If a single session key were used for multiple sessions, the data associated with all of them—potentially going back months—could become vulnerable. Because PFS-enabled configurations generate unique session keys for each new session, damage can be sharply limited. PFS is currently widely, but not universally, used with TLS.

That'll work well for websites using certificates issued by recognized CAs. But sometimes you might prefer to become your own CA and issue a private, self-signed certificate. This can sometimes work well for organizations that maintain internal websites accessed by team members spread around the world. Because you'd hope they'd all be willing to trust their own IT department, they don't need a CA certificate from a well-known organization.

The problem is that the browsers your team members use on their own computers won't know anything about your CA and, therefore, won't be able to establish secure connections with your organization's site. To make it work, you'll tell your users to click through the "Add Exception," "Proceed anyway," or "Continue to this website (not recommended)" warnings their browsers will display the first time they visit. This will cause the browser to add your self-signed certificate to its profile and should let your users sail right in the next time they visit.

What will your TLS certificate look like? The first thing to know is that it's a lightly formatted text file. The public key certificates used in TLS-powered connections are defined by the X.509 standard. The standard requires entries that include the identity of the subject (the machine or organization to whom the certificate was issued), the issuer (the CA), the start and end dates between which the certificate is valid, a serial number issued by the CA, and the public key itself (a hexadecimal string). Some certificates also include a subjectAltName value, which can include DNS names, email addresses, and IP addresses.

Listing 6.1: A sample self-signed root certificate (courtesy of Wikipedia: https:// en.wikipedia.org/wiki/X.509)

```
Certificate:
    Data:
        Version: 3 (0x2)
        Serial Number:
            04:00:00:00:00:01:15:4b:5a:c3:94
        Signature Algorithm: sha1WithRSAEncryption
        Issuer: C=BE, O=GlobalSign nv-sa, OU=Root CA, CN=GlobalSign Root CA
        Validity
            Not Before: Sep  1 12:00:00 1998 GMT
            Not After : Jan 28 12:00:00 2028 GMT
        Subject: C=BE, O=GlobalSign nv-sa, OU=Root CA, CN=GlobalSign Root CA
```

```
Subject Public Key Info:
    Public Key Algorithm: rsaEncryption
        Public-Key: (2048 bit)
        Modulus:
            00:da:0e:e6:99:8d:ce:a3:e3:4f:8a:7e:fb:f1:8b:
            ...
        Exponent: 65537 (0x10001)
    X509v3 extensions:
        X509v3 Key Usage: critical
            Certificate Sign, CRL Sign
        X509v3 Basic Constraints: critical
            CA:TRUE
        X509v3 Subject Key Identifier:
            60:7B:66:1A:45:0D:97:CA:89:50:2F:7D:04:CD:34:A8:FF:FC:FD:4B
Signature Algorithm: sha1WithRSAEncryption
    d6:73:e7:7c:4f:76:d0:8d:bf:ec:ba:a2:be:34:c5:28:32:b5:
    ...
```

Note how the value of `Validity` in that certificate states that the certificate will remain valid until January 28, 2028. That will be true unless the certificate is manually revoked before that date. This, for instance, might happen if there's a risk that the private key was compromised or if the associated domain is no longer active.

The CA responsible for the certificate will store the revocation notice in something called the *certificate revocation list* (CRL). Clients trying to access the server will automatically read the CRL and, if that certificate has indeed been revoked, will alert the user.

An alternate—and more efficient—method for checking for revocations involves querying a CA's Online Certificate Status Protocol (OCSP).

Generating Certificates

Once upon a time, some admins would avoid applying encryption to their websites because of the complexity. Creating error-free certificate signing requests (CSRs) was complicated and time-consuming. Others—particularly for smaller sites—might have been turned off by the fees charged by CAs. Thanks to a successful industry initiative, those are no longer valid excuses.

Since 2013, dozens of major technology companies have been working together to support the nonprofit Internet Security Research Group, whose mission is to "reduce financial, technological, and educational barriers to secure communication over the Internet." Their first project was the Let's Encrypt certificate authority (`https://letsencrypt.org`), which, as a CA, provides unlimited certificates at no cost.

The process of installing a Let's Encrypt certificate has, in some cases, been incorporated into the setup scripts of third-party platforms. But even if you run your own website, you can use the open-source Certbot tool to automate installation. Certbot is a project of the

Electronic Frontier Foundation that can also automate the renewal of Let's Encrypt certificates (that are valid for only 90 days). Figure 6.3 shows how you can tell the Certbot website (`https://certbot.eff.org`) what software you're running to display detailed instructions.

FIGURE 6.3   Installation instructions on the Certbot website

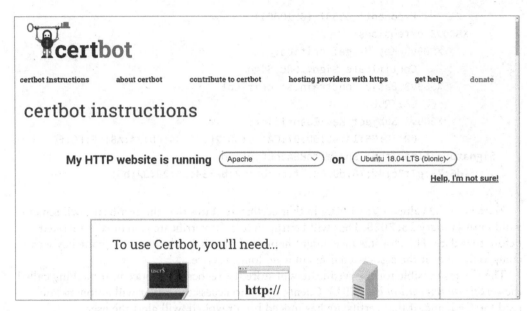

Installing Certbot itself takes only a couple of steps, while the complex operation of requesting, installing, and configuring your certificates requires (on an Ubuntu Linux server running Apache, at least) just this single command:

```
$ sudo certbot --apache
```

You'll be asked to identify the domains you want issued certificates for, and the software will handle all the details.

Email Encryption

Securing your web browsing activities is important, but those aren't the only things you do that can involve moving sensitive data across insecure networks. The security of email messages and the attachments you'll often include with them is at least as important to you and your organization, so you should be aware of some tools for encrypting them.

GNU Privacy Guard

GNU Privacy Guard (GPG or GnuPG) is software for securely encrypting files. GPG is compliant with OpenPGP systems. OpenPGP is, in turn, an open-source implementation of the restricted Pretty Good Privacy (PGP) program. This mess of standards, systems, and programs—not to mention acronyms—is the result of the evolution of the technology. PGP was originally released in the 1990s to be free for noncommercial use, but legal and, eventually, commercial considerations led to its privatization. OpenPGP is a standard defining the use of PGP encryption, and GPG was created as a free implementation of that standard.

Whichever flavor you go with, you'll use PGP to encrypt a file, with the goal of transferring it to a recipient who will decrypt and read it (using the private half of the public/private key pair). PGP will usually encrypt a file using the public key belonging to the recipient with a system that's not unlike the public key process we've already seen in use by TLS. OpenPGP standards-based encryption can be added to open-source email clients like Mozilla's Thunderbird running on any modern operating system by adding encryption extensions like Enigmail (`https://enigmail.net/index.php/en`).

An alternative encryption standard that's widely used in the corporate world is the proprietary Secure/Multipurpose Internet Mail Extensions (S/MIME). S/MIME controls data security, authentication, and message integrity.

With a valid license, you can install an S/MIME PKI certificate on the Thunderbird email client. Enterprise Google accounts allow you to configure Gmail to encrypt all outgoing messages using S/MIME.

Does Gmail Encrypt Your Emails?

Yes, they do. But, then again, they don't. Here's what I mean: Google most definitely applies TLS encryption to the emails it transmits between your account and other Gmail accounts or out to other TLS-compliant email providers. This is known as *transport encryption*. Some smaller private providers might not implement TLS, so communications with them will, obviously, not be protected.

But the encryption stops once an email arrives on Gmail servers. If that weren't true, then Gmail machines wouldn't be able to read your emails and apply spam and phishing attack filtering—not to mention offer you Smart Reply advice (or "serve" you advertisements). True end-to-end encryption is possible with Gmail browser clients by using a browser extension like FlowCrypt (`https://flowcrypt.com`) to encrypt messages before they reach Gmail servers.

Why might you want end-to-end encryption? Perhaps the attachments and information you include with your business or personal emails is highly sensitive and simply can't be exposed. Or perhaps you're not sure how reliable your email provider's privacy protocols are and you want to avoid experiencing a leak sometime down the line.

Google recently implemented something closer to end-to-end email encryption for their enterprise customers. But, for practical reasons, it still exposes some email header data.

Working with VPN Connections and Software Repositories

Virtual private networks (VPNs) and software repos aren't an obvious combination to string together in a single section, but I'll explain what they're doing here. First, just to make sure we're all on the same page, a VPN is a technique for extending a single private network across an insecure public network without compromising the security of the data moving back and forth. A software repository is an online site that hosts archives of software packages in a format that facilitates easy updates and downloads. Linux distributions are famous for providing easy access to curated software repositories containing many thousands of open-source software packages.

Now, despite their differences, what do they have in common? As I'm sure you've already guessed, they both benefit from obscuring data in transit through some kind of cryptography.

Securing Your Actions Using VPNs

In the case of VPNs, the goal is to hide your data from hostile eyes. Launching a VPN involves first establishing a secure network connection between your local network and a remote endpoint. Once established, the connection can be used as a *tunnel* through which your data is safely transferred. Popular technologies for creating the initial connection include OpenSSH, TLS, and Internet Protocol Security (IPsec). Figure 6.4 shows a simple VPN connection.

FIGURE 6.4   A typical VPN running through a secure tunnel connection

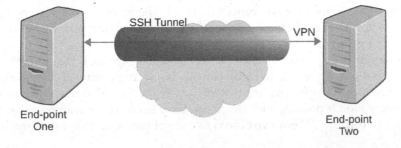

If you feel you can trust it, you can make use of one of the public VPN services available on the Internet. Or you can build your own using software like OpenVPN. Why go to all the bother in the first place? Here are some common use cases.

If you travel a lot and connect to the Internet through multiple public Wi-Fi access points, you may not want to expose your browsing activities across what might be insecure networks. Similarly, you might not fully trust your own Internet service provider to respect your right to privacy and properly protect your data.

In such cases, you'll want to use a VPN to anonymously log into a remote proxy server that will hide your activities from unauthorized eyes. A proxy server, by the way, is a server that stands between users and the Internet, or users and individual web services. The purpose of a proxy server is to route incoming or outgoing network traffic in ways that are more secure or more efficient than direct routing could provide. Technically, while VPNs are similar to proxy servers, they're built by default to provide robust, bidirectional encryption, something not universal to proxy servers.

You could also use a public VPN provider for such purposes rather than creating and maintaining your own, but just make sure that the provider itself is safe and reliable.

If your organization handles sensitive operations and data across multiple geographic locations, you may need a way for your team members to safely connect to each other and access resources remotely. Establishing VPN connections between your remote sites is, when properly configured, an excellent way to do this.

If you're not sure how the data generated by your gaming consoles or smart TVs is handled by their vendors, you can configure a home router with a VPN that will mask data in transit and at least partially control how it's used. Such VPNs can also allow users to circumvent geographic restrictions on accessing content. Note that using VPNs for this purpose could break local laws or contract conditions.

Securing Transfers from Software Repositories

For software repositories the problem is ensuring that the package you end up installing on your local system is the same as the official version that's been living on the online repo. What could go wrong? Well, consider what actually happened to the Linux Mint project some years back where its website was temporarily hacked and a download image was replaced with a fake. A small number of people ended up downloading and installing a dangerous OS before the problem was noticed and fixed (which, because of an alert website admin team, happened soon after the breach).

Here's an example of how cryptography can help. On the Linux Debian software repository system used by more than a few distributions—including Ubuntu—a software archive will contain text files listing the correct checksums (which are similar to hashes). Those checksums should match the actual values you get by generating checksums from the other archive files. If the supplied and actual checksums don't match, then you'll know someone's been tampering with your package, and you shouldn't trust it. Even during the Linux Mint hack, users who took the time to compare the checksums would have known something was wrong.

You don't have to use exactly this solution to secure your transfers. Git-based distributed version control repositories like GitHub (https://github.com), for instance, ensure the validity of the software and other data you're transferring through either SSH or TLS (HTTPS) connections.

Summary

When given a choice, always work with encrypted options (like SSH and HTTPS) rather than unencrypted software (like Telnet and HTTP).

When data is sent in plain text across insecure networks, it is readable to anyone connected to the network who might be listening. Encryption obscures the data so that, for all practical purposes, it can't be read without access to the decryption key.

Most website encryption is managed by well-known certificate authorities, but smaller or internal networks will sometimes use their own private self-signed certificates, assuming that their own team will know to trust the site.

The Let's Encrypt project makes free encryption certificates available, along with a simple, automated installation process.

Email messages and attachments can be encrypted end-to-end by using extensions like Enigmail (with Mozilla's Thunderbird) and FlowCrypt (for Gmail).

Access to online software sources—called *repositories*—should be protected by some form of cryptographic security to ensure the packages you're downloading haven't been altered. Checksums (which are, effectively, hashes) are often used as part of this process.

Exam Essentials

Understand how website encryption works.   A certificate authority issues a certificate for the site that, when it's installed, will be used to confirm to client browsers that the site is encrypted. Session keys are generated based on the certificate and used throughout the ensuing session.

Understand the role and basic structure of TLS X.509 certificates.   A certificate following the X.509 standard will contain entries identifying the scope (start and end dates) and ownership (issuer and subject) of the certificate, along with serial numbers and the hexadecimal strings defining the public key itself.

Understand the basics of file encryption.   Encryption software using the PGP standard encrypts an object using the recipient's public key so that only someone in possession of the private version of that key will be able to decrypt it.

Understand how VPNs are used to protect your activities from interception on insecure networks.   A VPN is a way to extend a secure local network across an untrusted area to a remote network. Typically, you will first establish a secure connection using an underlying technology like SSH, which you'll use as a tunnel for your VPN activities.

Review Questions

1. Within the context of encryption, the data that populates the page of a website is most accurately referred to as what?

   A. Data in transit

   B. Static data

   C. Data at rest

   D. Dynamic data

2. Which of these acronyms represents a protocol that's used to deliver encrypted web pages?

   A. VPN

   B. SFTP

   C. HTTPS

   D. HTTP

3. How can you be (relatively) sure that a website you're visiting uses data encryption? (Choose two.)

   A. Your browser will display a text-based confirmation toward the top of the page.

   B. The URL address will begin with `https`.

   C. The page's text content will be displayed by your browser in a darker, bolder font.

   D. No prominent warnings and security alerts will be displayed by your browser when you try to load the page.

4. What is the role root certificates play in browser security?

   A. A root certificate will prevent your browser from loading unencrypted web pages.

   B. A root certificate installed on the servers of a certificate authority (CA) is used to validate browser requests globally.

   C. A root certificate included in a browser package is used to identify the presence of a valid CA-issued certificate on the server.

   D. A root certificate installed on a web server is used to confirm the status of a client browser.

5. What is the primary task of the Let's Encrypt project?

   A. To research new and better website encryption methodologies

   B. To maintain statistics on the global adoption of website encryption

   C. To make information about the importance of encryption certificates as widely available as possible

   D. To make TLS encryption certificates freely available as widely as possible

6. What technology can be used to prevent session keys being improperly reused to access protected data without authentication?

   A. GNU Privacy Guard

   B. OpenPGP

   C. Perfect forward secrecy

   D. HTTPS

7. Which of the following can be considered plain-text protocols? (Choose two.)

   A. FTP

   B. HTTP

   C. SSH

   D. HTTPS

8. What functionality does an SSL server test come to measure?

   A. The effectiveness of an email server's encryption configuration

   B. The reliability of the name servers used by the website domain

   C. The validity of the website's initial certificate request

   D. The effectiveness of a website's encryption configuration

9. What is OpenPGP?

   A. A commercial implementation of the use of PGP encryption

   B. An open-source standard for implementing the PGP standard

   C. An open-source implementation of the GPG standard

   D. A secure email client software package

10. What is a third-party tool for achieving end-to-end encryption for your Gmail emails?

    A. FlowCrypt

    B. GPG

    C. TLS

    D. Thunderbird

11. What is a VPN?

    A. A network topography that protects private networks from external infiltration

    B. A software package that secures the remote transfer and installation of applications

    C. A technique for safely extending a single private network across an insecure public network

    D. The software equivalent of a firewall

12. What best describes a network tunnel?

    A. A "network within a network" that permits simultaneous duplex transmissions

    B. A wired network extension that physically connects resources in multiple facilities

    C. A common way to describe a virtual private network

    D. An existing secure remote network connection that can be utilized by secondary processes

13. How can you be sure that a software package you downloaded wasn't altered or substituted in transit?

    A. By comparing the checksum value on the source website with a checksum you generate on the downloaded file

    B. By only getting your software from reliable sources

    C. By testing your new software for malware before installing it

    D. By using a firewall to shut down your network connection while downloading the software

Chapter

7

Risk Assessment

THE LPI SECURITY ESSENTIALS EXAM OBJECTIVES COVERED IN THIS CHAPTER MAY INCLUDE, BUT ARE NOT LIMITED TO, THE FOLLOWING:

✓ **021.2 Risk assessment and management**

- Know common sources for security information

- Understanding of security incident classification schema and important types of security vulnerabilities

- Understanding of the concepts of security assessments and IT forensics

✓ **021.3 Ethical behavior**

- Awareness of legal implications of security scans, assessments, and attacks

When we teach the topic of risk management to IT professionals, what we're really doing is showing them how to break into private systems, grab private data, and inflict maximum chaos and mayhem on as many private resources as possible.

Wait.

Is openly teaching such dangerous skills really a good idea? You bet it is. Because this is the best—and perhaps only—way to prepare admins to protect their systems from the attacks that, sooner or later, they're certainly going to face.

In fact, regularly staging aggressive cyber attacks against your own infrastructure is so important that it's often *required* before your business can be certified as reliable enough to operate within certain industries. Your bank, for instance, may not let you directly process credit card payments through your website until you can successfully pass an audit using Payment Card Industry Data Security Standard (PCI-DSS) objectives—objectives that include regularly testing security systems and processes.

A full IT risk assessment will help you understand your system's weaknesses, but getting there will require working through a few steps. You'll need to do the following:

1. Scan the Internet for publicly available information that could potentially be used against your infrastructure (open-source intelligence [OSINT] gathering).

2. Assemble an up-to-date database of known vulnerability definitions.

3. Use those definitions to scan your infrastructure for potential software or configuration vulnerabilities (vulnerability testing).

4. See if you can gain access to your infrastructure using unauthorized means (penetration testing).

While no one working with digital resources should ever lose sight of the threat landscape, performing full vulnerability and penetration scans is often left to specialists. Many organizations will hire outside consultants for the job. This is partly because they're the ones with more practical experience and the necessary industry certifications, but it's also because the best way to know how vulnerable you are is to see if someone with little or no "inside" information can beat your defenses.

Many established companies actually encourage outsiders to try to penetrate their defenses and then submit full reports. In many cases, such companies will even offer cash rewards for discoveries of significant vulnerabilities. Those rewards are often called *bug bounties*. Before attempting such a scan, however, be sure to confirm you're operating well within the program rules and limits.

But whoever ends up testing your security posture, you should at least be aware of the basic principles and tools of the trade. Those are the grapes we'll be fermenting for the rest of this chapter.

Conducting Open-Source Intelligence Gathering

You won't believe how much sensitive information about your organization is sitting on the public Internet right now waiting to be discovered. And you won't believe who it was who put it there. Spoiler alert: it was you (and the people you work with).

Suppose your company's e-commerce web application is built from a secret sauce made up of a complicated mix of technologies. The whole thing is strung together with a software platform that's not widely used. That, you figure, makes things more secure, because it'll be much harder for potential hackers to guess which skills they'll need to do their damage. To further protect your security and competitive advantage, your company is careful not to publish too many details about how the application works under the hood. And, of course, all the admins and developers had to sign one of those 25-page nondisclosure agreements before being shown the crown jewels.

So, you'd think you'd be in pretty good shape, confidentiality-wise. And you'd probably be wrong. Remember the most recent round of hiring you went through last summer? Weren't you the one who spent a whole morning carefully crafting that LinkedIn ad for the two new developers you were after? I'm sure it's coming back to you now, especially the part where you list all the technologies you wanted your developers to have previously worked with. Think about how you made sure that the list included every single ingredient in your (formerly) secret sauce?

This is what an open-source intelligence hacker does. With nothing more than the name of your company and a LinkedIn account, someone could search through your company's account history for job ads and vacuum out whatever is useful.

What else is out there? Does your hacker know the names of some members of your team? Is it possible that those names can be associated with active Stack Overflow or Reddit accounts? Would it be difficult to search through those platforms to see what can be learned from conversations relating to problems or clever solutions your developers were working on?

Think that's scary? Just wait till you hear about some of the freely available automated reconnaissance tools that exist. Recon-ng, for example, lets you provide some basic identifying details (like a company name and website) and then heads out to the Internet on its own to see what can be found. The software already knows all the tricks and can cover more ground in a couple of minutes than you could in a month.

The point of all this isn't to teach you how to attack other people's websites. Tim Tomes, Recon-ng's creator, isn't some creepy hacker who hasn't showered in two months; he is a widely respected and successful Internet security expert who fights for the good guys. The real goal of these tools is to help you rebuild your organization's security posture so other people can't hack you. Knowing how easy it is to discover so much about your organization should inspire you to tighten things up and, perhaps, change the way you present yourself to the world.

Besides the open-source Recon-ng (`https://github.com/lanmaster53/recon-ng`), other OSINT tools include Maltego (`www.maltego.com`—proprietary with a limited-use community edition), the Shodan search engine (`www.shodan.io`—some free access available), the image search tool TinEye (`www.tineye.com`), and a clever use of search engines known as Google Dorks (see `https://en.wikipedia.org/wiki/Google_hacking`).

Accessing Public Vulnerability Databases

In the next section, we're going to talk about running vulnerability scans against your infrastructure. Now "running scans" is all well and good, but how useful will that be if you don't really know what it is you're looking for? It sounds a bit like hiring someone to keep watch over your house while you're away on vacation but neglecting to share your address. So here's where I'll show you how to find and use some very large, publicly available databases filled with acres and acres of vulnerability definition goodness.

A vulnerability, as we saw back in Chapter 2 ("What Are Vulnerabilities and Threats?"), is any misconfiguration, oversight, or hole in your defenses that could allow a security breach. Considering that there are tens of thousands of known vulnerabilities already out there—with hundreds more being discovered every month—would you even know where to start looking?

Because data and infrastructure security is such a critical matter, a number of publicly funded security organizations maintain databases of vulnerability definitions that can be fed into and used by scanning software systems. When properly updated, you can relatively quickly check your operating systems, configurations, running services, and networks for problems. More important, you can automate the process so scans are run every week or month and so you're instantly alerted if serious problems are detected.

But for the results to be useful, you'll need to understand how the definitions are classified. To understand that, you'll need to be familiar with who's collecting them and how they're managed. Before we begin, though, I should warn you that there are some pretty serious acronyms coming, like SCAP, ARF, CPE, SCE, CVSS, and TMSAD. Proceed with appropriate caution.

Vulnerability Data Frameworks

It begins with the U.S. government's National Vulnerability Database (NVD), a project of the National Institute of Standards and Technology (NIST). NVD serves as a "repository of standards based vulnerability management data represented using the Security Content Automation Protocol (SCAP)"—see `https://nvd.nist.gov`. NIST maintains a dashboard on its website at `https://nvd.nist.gov/general/nvd-dashboard` where you can view current statistics on vulnerability definitions arranged by category. Figure 7.1 shows the NVD Dashboard.

FIGURE 7.1   The NVD Dashboard

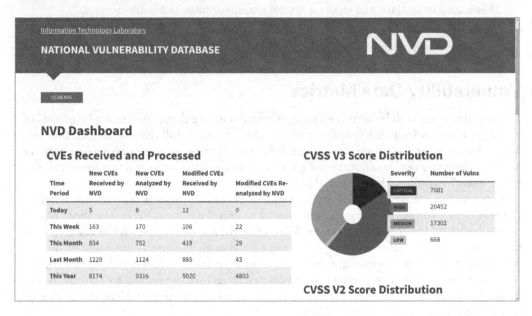

The SCAP framework is a collection of standards and protocols that can be applied to creating and managing automated vulnerability scanning and measurement. In English, that means SCAP supports a set of tools that organizations can freely use within their own infrastructure to regularly monitor their systems for the presence of vulnerabilities. The SCAP framework acts as an organizing structure for all the moving parts responsible for collecting, categorizing, and distributing new and existing vulnerability definitions and for launching scan operations against private infrastructure. SCAP is a free service available to anyone, anywhere.

Besides SCAP, the Open Web Application Security Project (OWASP—https://owasp.org) is an excellent source of information and tools relating to security assessments.

Vulnerability Data Formats

SCAP work involves boatloads of regularly updated data that'll be used widely across unpredictable environments. To keep everything manageable, you'll want to standardize that data using some carefully designed formats. Here are some of the key formats commonly in use:

- **Common Vulnerabilities and Exposures (CVE):** The CVE is a naming standard for security vulnerabilities and exposures. A CVE name is assigned to each vulnerability and serves as its identifier, especially when used within an implementation platform.

- **Common Platform Enumeration (CPE):** A CPE value is used as part of a vulnerability definition document to identify a vulnerability's target operating system and installed software packages. For example, cpe:/o:fedoraproject:fedora:22 is an identifier pointing to the Fedora Linux OS.

- **Open Vulnerability and Assessment Language (OVAL):** OVAL is a declarative language that's used to contain and report a system's configuration and security state.
- **Asset Reporting Format (ARF):** ARF can be used to consolidate multiple OVAL result files into a single data stream.

Vulnerability Data Metrics

The two problems with boatloads of autogenerated data are that (1) there are boatloads of it and (2) it makes for mind-numbingly dull reading. It's such dull reading, in fact, that you will definitely want your computer to read it for you. While your computer will be only too happy to help you out, you'll still need a way to consume the results in some format or the whole exercise will have been for nothing.

Vulnerability scanners can present their output as alerts or reports that provide quick summaries in a format that's easy to consume. The most important element of those reports is the consistent use of a scoring system. What, exactly, are we scoring? While it's common for a scan to uncover dozens of vulnerabilities on a system, as often as not, most of those will be the result of minor configuration choices or even false positives. To help you focus your attention on the most pressing security holes, results will be ranked by severity. A bug that's already been the target of active exploits and gets a score of 9 or 10 might be clearly marked in the output display in bright red.

How does the metric work? The Common Vulnerability Scoring System (CVSS) will assign a vulnerability score for each of a number of factors. If, for instance, the chances of a particular vulnerability being exploited are high—meaning that it's relatively easy for hackers to find and abuse the weakness—then the score will rise. Similarly, if an exploit will likely lead to a significant negative impact on your system's operations, the score will go up further. Any total score above 7 or so should attract your prompt attention.

Vulnerability Data Management Tools

You can directly download NVD data from the NVD website (`https://nvd.nist.gov/vuln/data-feeds`). But that probably won't do you a lot of good. After all, who wants to manually read through hundreds of megabytes of JavaScript Object Notation (JSON) data on a computer screen? And in any case, the NVD feed is scheduled to be retired in late 2023.

Instead, you'll be far more likely to install software to regularly—and invisibly— synchronize the data you've already got with the latest updates from the NVD collection. That software can then use the latest data as part of local scans. Packages for handling those tasks include OpenSCAP, OpenVAS, and Nessus.

The next part of the chapter will describe the vulnerability scanning process. But first, to provide you with a visualization of the complete vulnerability tool ecosystem, Figure 7.2 illustrates the relationships between various standards, protocols, and tools.

FIGURE 7.2   A layered diagram of NVD-related tools

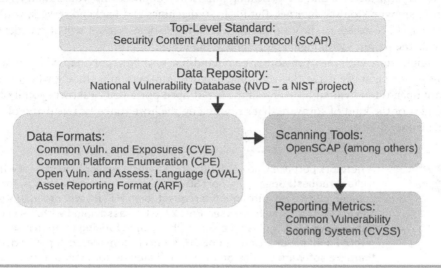

As of October 2019, the old Extensible Markup Language (XML) vulnerability data feeds were retired in favor of JSON feeds. JSON feeds offer more data points and greater accuracy.

Conducting Vulnerability Scans

At the edges, there will be some overlap between vulnerability scanning and penetration testing. Their ultimate goals are the same and they'll often use some of the same tools. But at the core, *scanning* is about using NVD definitions to discover vulnerabilities, while *pen testing* is designed to see how far those vulnerabilities can actually be exploited. So here we'll talk about passive scanning and save all the dirty, black hat stuff for the next section.

For a lot of reasons, you—or the IT security specialist you hire—will probably use either a new purpose-built laptop or a clean virtual machine for your scanning. For one thing, you don't want to risk contaminating your results with anything that might have been left on the machine from a previous job. Besides, you really don't want to risk contaminating your machine with any of the dark monsters that might be living on the machines you're scanning.

Because Linux is so good at virtualization and because scanning software tends to feel especially at home on Linux, Linux will probably be your base of operations. In fact, there are Linux distributions—like Kali Linux—that come already optimized for security operations and pre-loaded with many of the software tools you'll need.

A vulnerability scan will normally be run from a computer that's independent of the equipment you're targeting. Having said that, you will need network access on some level.

If you're targeting servers that are providing public web applications, you should be able to scan from anywhere on the Internet. But for local machines and backend servers, you'll at least have to have access to the local network (LAN). In some cases, it will also make sense to provide the scanner with login credentials to the target.

You might start with the open-source command-line tool Nmap. Nmap will scan a network host—or an entire network—returning detailed information including which network ports are open on individual hosts. From the list of open ports you're shown, you'll often get a good idea of the kind of software that's running on the host you've scanned and of some possible vulnerabilities.

A network port is a kind of identifier that tells a server how to deal with a client request. Specifying port 80 along with a network address, for instance, tells the host to send the request to an HTTP server to load a website in the client's web browser. Port 22, when associated with the same network address, will tell the server that you're looking to open a secure remote connection using OpenSSH. A port is considered "open" when there's a software service on the server listening for incoming requests. You "close" a port by shutting down that software.

Some software packages bundle the functionality of a full range of scanning tools including Nmap. The products in this market, which include OpenVAS, Nessus, Nexpose, and Burp Suite, tend to be commercial, but will usually have lighter "community editions" available. Greenbone's open-source edition OpenVAS is an exception, in that there are no restrictions on its use. Besides the commercial-based products, the OpenSCAP project (www.open-scap.org) is entirely free.

All of those packages provide a GUI interface, relatively intuitive configuration controls, and sophisticated reporting options. They'll survey what's running in your target network, whether server software like Apache, WordPress, and PHP are installed and active and, most important, whether there are any visible configuration problems or unpatched vulnerabilities.

A full scan can actually consume enough network bandwidth to force legitimate processes down. Always confirm in advance that what you're planning to do is safe and permitted.

While all vulnerability scanners will provide detailed reports of their scans, the results might not be identical. You might need to test more than one tool on your infrastructure, so, based on your results, you can decide which one is best suited for your needs or work to fine-tune your scan configurations.

Conducting Penetration Tests

With the data acquired from a solid round of vulnerability scans under your belt, you're ready to try to break into your target system and do some damage.

But before you push that big red button, you should consider reasons why that might *not* be a great idea. For one thing, if you launch pen testing tools against a target without explicit, written authorization from the owners, you can be criminally liable. Agents in dark suits tend to get touchy about digital trespass. Even more to the point: if you're not very careful, you could do some real and irreversible damage to your target without being aware of it (and find yourself on the hook for significant financial compensation claims). Finally, not every use-case scenario necessarily calls for pen testing; sometimes a vulnerability scan is everything the doctor ordered.

But once you've carefully defined the scope of your operation, got all the legalities out of the way, and decided to take your testing to the next level, you'll need to settle on the combination of attack types you'll need.

Attack Vectors

There's no end to the ingenuity and creativity displayed by hackers eager to get to your digital valuables. But here are some of the popular approaches you should both understand and be ready to emulate as part of a pen test:

- **Phishing**: Can you directly phone or email someone in your organization and request confidential content (like authentication information) by claiming to be someone you're not? If you can do that, then you've got your ticket into the system.

- **Unauthorized Physical Access**: By this I mean a good, old-fashioned game of *break and enter*. How easy is it to gain access to your target's servers and networking hardware? If you're able to just walk into a server room without attracting anyone's attention, it'll be dead easy to plug in a cheap USB malware or sniffer device or install a backdoor.

- **SQL Injection**: A poorly configured database-consuming front end intended to support a website can, once discovered, be used to steal or destroy your organization's private data. Testing the technique is trivial (but then so is preventing it by properly configuring your website).

- **Man-in-the-Middle Attacks**: Unencrypted remote communications can be intercepted and altered by anyone with access to the network. A pen tester who discovers such a session can impersonate either end of the session and insert unintended responses, corrupting data and possibly eliciting sensitive information.

- **Cross-Site Scripting (XSS)**: Vulnerable web pages can be injected with malicious client-side scripts, potentially giving attackers elevated privileges (a form of privilege escalation) where they shouldn't have them.

- **Buffer Overflows**: Poorly written programs can sometimes permit writes to system memory beyond the memory areas (or "buffers") assigned to them. This could be exploited by malicious website visitors to execute unrelated—and potentially damaging—processes.

Tooling Frameworks

Some of the attack vectors mentioned in the previous section don't require any special tools. Phishing, for instance, just takes some basic information about your target and a bit of ingenuity. Unauthorized physical access requires only a pair of feet (and a cheeky attitude). But making a serious and complete challenge is going to have to include a far wider range of attacks, many of which being technically demanding. For this, most people will need help in the form of an exploit platform.

The security community supports a number of frameworks built to guide you through the attack process. The OWASP project mentioned earlier provides the OWASP Zed Attack Proxy (ZAP) that you can use against a web application. In addition, the security company Rapid7 stands behind the Metasploit Project, which includes tools for executing exploits against susceptible remote machines.

Needless to say, it's expected that such tools—created and maintained by ethical and legitimate organizations—may be used only for ethical and legitimate purposes. That means you're allowed to run them only against your own property for security testing purposes, and not for any other goal.

You should also be aware of red team/blue team exercises, which are an extreme form of penetration testing pitting teams of administrators and security professionals against each other. The blue team is tasked with defending a defined infrastructure stack, while the red team attempts to penetrate the system and achieve a preset objective. The realistic, real-time nature of such "war games" is an excellent way to develop and improve security skills.

Follow-Up

Once the intelligence gathering, vulnerability scanning, enumeration, and exploitation phases are over, your job won't be complete until you perform an impact analysis and, if there are other principals involved, submit a report. The impact analysis is to ensure that you fully understand what happened, what weaknesses exist in your infrastructure, what has to be fixed, and how you should prioritize your efforts. The report should provide a clear review of the operation using language that will make sense to all the individuals who are meant to read it. Maintaining an archive of testing reports can offer you both an ongoing historical context for your operations and a good foundation for later compliance and regulatory needs.

In other words, make sure you keep up with your paperwork.

Summary

You can't properly understand how secure your infrastructure is without testing it against realistic, simulated attacks.

Open-source intelligence gathering searches public networks for compromising information about your organization.

Recon-ng is an example of a software suite that effectively automates the OSINT process.

Vulnerability scanning tools use definitions curated and maintained in U.S. government-sponsored databases. It would be pretty much impossible to effectively scan your infrastructure without using those definitions.

The Common Vulnerability Scoring System (CVSS) is used to alert you to more urgent vulnerabilities that have been discovered on your system.

Vulnerability scanning and penetration testing are complex, multistep tasks that require careful preparation and solid skills. They're often performed by third-party consultants.

It's critical to obtain written permission from the owners of a target infrastructure before scanning and to avoid breaking any laws or causing unnecessary damage.

Exam Essentials

Be aware of the value of OSINT and some common tools for gathering it.   You and your organization probably leave much more compromising information on the Internet than you realize. Regularly running automated intel gathering tools to show you what's out there can help you fill holes and improve your processes.

Be aware of available stores of updated databases of vulnerability definitions.   The National Vulnerability Database (NVD) maintains and hosts vulnerability data formatted using the SCAP protocol to be compatible with automated vulnerability scanning operations.

Understand the formats, protocols, and scoring systems used for vulnerability definitions.   The Common Vulnerabilities and Exposures (CVE) determines how vulnerabilities are named, the Common Platform Enumeration (CPE) is used to identify the host OS and installed software, the Open Vulnerability and Assessment Language (OVAL) is used to report a host's state, and the Common Vulnerability Scoring System (CVSS) is used to highlight particularly serious vulnerabilities.

Be aware of the tools available for vulnerability scanning and penetration testing.   Kali Linux is a distribution that's preconfigured with the settings and tools you're likely to need. Nmap, OpenVAS, Nessus, Nexpose, Burp Suite, and OpenSCAP are all useful scanning tools. The OWASP Zed Attack Proxy (ZAP) and the Metasploit Project are particularly suited for penetration testing.

Be aware of common attack vectors that might be directed against your infrastructure.   Phishing attacks seek to fool people into disclosing private information. A lot can be gained (and lost) through unauthorized physical access. SQL injection, man-in-the-middle, and cross-site scripting attacks are often used to illegally acquire or damage private data.

Review Questions

1. What is the best way to describe the process of searching publicly available data collections for your organization's sensitive information?

   A. Hacking

   B. OSINT reconnaissance

   C. Vulnerability testing

   D. Penetration testing

2. Which of the following tools are designed specifically for OSINT operations? (Choose two.)

   A. Google dorks

   B. Recon-ng

   C. Maltego

   D. FireEye

3. From a privacy perspective, what makes LinkedIn so potentially dangerous?

   A. Companies and employees often reveal too many details about their work.

   B. The site administrators have access to authentication information.

   C. Live, dynamic links between LinkedIn and your on-site data stores can sometimes leak sensitive data.

   D. Former employees can easily post unauthorized sensitive data.

4. What is the role of the National Vulnerability Database (NVD)?

   A. It is a repository of standards-based vulnerability management data.

   B. It is a source of information and tools relating to security assessments.

   C. It is an organizing structure for the collecting, categorizing, and distributing vulnerability definitions.

   D. It is a naming standard for security vulnerabilities and exposures.

5. What is the role of the Common Platform Enumeration (CPE)?

   A. A declarative language that's used to contain and report a system's configuration and security state

   B. A format for consolidating multiple OVAL result files into a single data stream

   C. A repository of standards-based vulnerability management data

   D. A standard for identifying a vulnerability's target operating system and software profile

6. How do vulnerability scanners "know" how to rank the severity of the vulnerabilities they find on your system?

   A. They apply artificial intelligence and machine learning.

   B. They use the Asset Reporting Format (ARF).

   C. They use the Common Vulnerability Scoring System (CVSS).

   D. They don't. Their job is only to report what they find and leave assessment up to you.

7. Where would you normally acquire vulnerability definitions data?

   A. Definitions are installed by default on all modern operating systems.

   B. Definitions are loaded by vulnerability scanners as part of the setup process.

   C. Definitions can be downloaded from the U.S. government's National Vulnerability Database (NVD).

   D. Definitions can be downloaded from the Open Web Application Security Project website.

8. What data format is currently used by vulnerability definitions?

   A. XML

   B. JSON

   C. YAML

   D. MD

9. Which of the following vulnerability testing packages is open source? (Choose two.)

   A. SCAP

   B. Nexpose

   C. OpenVAS

   D. Nessus

10. What best describes the primary goal of a vulnerability scan?

    A. To catalog the complete current set of known vulnerabilities

    B. To discover unresolved vulnerabilities in an organization's network or devices

    C. To discover how easily existing defenses can be breached

    D. To see whether it's possible to reach and/or destroy an organization's data without proper authentication

11. What is a network port?

    A. A numeric identifier that permits targeted routing to multiple services using a single IP address

    B. A physical cable connector controlling traffic within a network

    C. The private IP address assigned to a local device

    D. A firewall that can, when needed, be used to shut down access to a network

12. What should precede all penetration test operations? (Choose two.)

    A. A full vulnerability scan

    B. Explicit written permission from the infrastructure owners

    C. Prior knowledge of security login information from the infrastructure owners

    D. Prior knowledge of the digital assets held on the infrastructure

13. How would you describe an attack launched through a poorly configured web application front end?

    A. Man in the middle

    B. Cross-site scripting

    C. Phishing

    D. SQL injection

14. How would you describe an attack that's executed by intercepting data in transit between remote locations?

    A. Phishing

    B. Man in the middle

    C. SQL injection

    D. Physical infiltration

15. What elements should be included in a risk assessment's final report? (Choose three.)

    A. Inventory of existing infrastructure weaknesses

    B. An estimate of the potential costs to the organization of various attack scenarios

    C. Itemized list of needed changes

    D. Review of each of the assessment's steps

Chapter

8

Configuring System Backups and Monitoring

THE LPI SECURITY ESSENTIALS EXAM OBJECTIVES COVERED IN THIS CHAPTER MAY INCLUDE, BUT ARE NOT LIMITED TO, THE FOLLOWING:

✓ **023.4 Data availability**

- Understanding of the importance of backups

- Understanding of common backup types and strategies

- Understanding of the security implications of backups

- Creating and securely storing backups

- Understanding of data storage, access, and sharing in cloud services

- Understanding of the security implications of cloud storage and shared access in the cloud

- Awareness of the dependence on Internet connection and the synchronization of data between cloud services and local storage

"If you've got data, then you'd better make sure you've also got a robust and practical plan for backing it up." I'm sure you've heard that one before. I'm equally sure that it didn't catch you by surprise: this isn't news to anyone doing the things we all do. But wait? Isn't this book about security? What does *that* have to do with data backups?

There are a lot of reasons for addressing backups here, but if you had to limit yourself to just one, the following common and timely scenario would be it.

Imagine you're responsible for the IT systems powering the municipal services for your small town. Without those computers and their data, municipal workers won't get paid next month, the local library won't know where any of their books are, the 911 emergency service communication system's phones won't ring, and the town's information website will go offline.

Now imagine that one fine morning you log into the main server and you're greeted by the cheerful news that all the data on your systems has been encrypted by a hacker from Eastern Europe and that they won't give you the decryption key to restore your access unless you pay them a couple hundred thousand dollars' worth of cryptocurrency. Don't think this is realistic? Major hospitals, utilities, and entire small cities have been brought to their knees by just such attacks.

What are your choices?

- You could pay the ransom and hope the attackers keep their promise to decrypt your data. But, historically, they often haven't. Criminals aren't known for being honest.

- You could try using decryption tools provided by major security companies and government agencies (like https://noransom.kaspersky.com) and hope that they'll work on your system. This is certainly a valid option, but it won't work in all cases.

- You could wipe your systems clean and rebuild everything from scratch. This could be hugely expensive and take months to complete.

But do you know how you can stop the attack cold and walk away virtually untouched? If you had complete, up-to-date backup copies of your systems (both the user data and the application systems themselves), then all you'll need to do is rebuild from your backups. Worst case, you're down for an hour or two and few people even notice. Even better, you could plan things really well by designing an always running "hot" backup infrastructure that's preconfigured to go live the minute the main system goes down. It's known as *failover*, and it's the kind of plan that can make you a big hero and earn you a big raise.

Still not sure what backups have to do with security?

Let's see how it all works.

Why You Need to Get Backups Right the First Time

Let's imagine a different way our ransomware scenario could have played out. Looking up from the screen displaying the hackers' threat, you comment to your assistant that "It sure is a good thing we're all backed up here. We'd better get to work restoring the system." Suppose one of these happens next:

- You realize that you haven't actually performed a full backup for six months. The data you've got is too old to be useful.

- You originally set a schedule for regular backups, but you realize that your assistant just didn't get around to creating one since last March.

- Your latest backup is quite recent, but you realize that data from critical databases wasn't included. You'll have your system back, but you'll have no idea how much money to pay your teachers and ambulance drivers or, for that matter, what their names are and how you're supposed to deposit funds into their bank accounts. You're not even sure how to access the city's own back account.

- All critical data is intact, but the custom-built software solutions that consume it were never backed up.

- Your backup protocol was perfect and covered everything you need, but, as you begin the restore operation, you realize the backup media drives have failed. It's not recoverable. You wisely decide not to return the mayor's phone calls. Perhaps now is a good time to head out on that vacation you've been planning.

It's not good enough just backing up "stuff." You have to make sure you get *all the stuff*. And it's not helpful to do it once in a while. When things go bad, you'll need to be able to quickly restore your system to a *working* state, which obviously must include the latest data collected from recent transactions.

How "quick" is quick enough, and how "complete" is complete enough? That will depend on your organization's operational needs. It's common for administrators to measure their needs in terms of a recovery point objective (RPO) and recovery time objective (RTO). An RPO is the system state you need to be able to recover that will be current enough for your organization's minimum requirements. So, for instance, if your recovered system will have data that includes all but the last hour preceding the crash, you'll be able to get by. But a loss of *two* hours of data would be catastrophic; the financial or reputation loss you'd face would be too serious. For such an organization, you'd better make sure you have an RPO of one hour or less.

An RTO, on the other hand, is a measure of how soon you need to get your system back up and running at full speed before really bad things start happening to your organization. By way of example, suppose your e-commerce site was offline for 12 hours. You'll lose some business, obviously, but your business analysts tell you that anything up to 48 hours is still livable. More than 48 hours, however, and customers will assume you're down for good and head over to the competition (which, all things being equal, will be Amazon).

Therefore, when you plan your backup regimen, you'll take both the RPO and RTO into account. You'll need to make sure a new backup is run within the RPO (say, one hour) and also make sure you can access your backup archives and successfully restore the data to the applications in less than the RTO (48 hours, in our example).

This kind of planning is hugely important for "getting backups right." But there will be other considerations, too. Let's explore.

Appreciating the Risks

So what, exactly, is at stake in the backup game? Not generating regular backups can leave you vulnerable to ransomware, as you've seen, but also to a horror show of other potential nightmares. Just think what might happen to your organization as a result of a catastrophic fire or similar disruption. Are there enough resources located a safe distance from your building that you could use to rebuild in an emergency? That question is just as valid—and just as scary—when asked about a serious theft: could you recover from the sudden loss of all your computers?

Having trouble getting to sleep at night because you're worried about that kind of disaster scenario? Well, it doesn't have to be so dramatic, you know. Imagine what would happen if a new admin or developer accidentally wiped out your main database. If you haven't worked with databases, you'll have no clue how easy that would be. If you *have* worked with databases, you probably drift peacefully off to sleep at night by thinking about fires, tornadoes, and theft...anything to get your mind off database errors.

I'm sure you're seeing the pattern, here. If you don't yet have a solid backup plan in place, start working on one right now. Already have a good plan? I'll bet you're feeling pretty good about yourself right now.

Bad move.

Here's why. What physical media are you backing up to? High-density hard drives? DVDs? Tape drives? Did you know that backup drives of all types are notorious for failing, and usually at the worst possible time? Any given drive might keep running for a decade, but there's also no way to be sure it won't fail tomorrow. And even if they keep spinning, digital data archives can degrade over long periods of time. Once even the smallest sector of a digital archive is no longer reliable, you can assume the worst about your ability to retrieve the rest.

Even if your storage media does survive the ravages of time, are you sure you'll be able to read it years from now? Perhaps, just like you're unlikely to find a working 5.25″ floppy disk drive to retrieve your 30-year-old data archives, you may similarly have trouble accessing data from today's storage drive technologies 30 years ahead. As hard as the pace of change in the technology world might make it, planning far enough ahead to match your goals is essential.

The bottom line is that you should never trust a *single* storage device with an important backup. And you should never trust your backups to a *single* location. Aiming for at least some level of built-in redundancy will significantly improve the security of your data.

Spreading Your Backups Across Multiple Sites

Given that distributing your backup archives across multiple locations can greatly improve your chances of surviving a major incident, it's worth spending some time looking at some practical options. Broadly speaking, either you could regularly write archives to a local physical drive and transport the drive to a remote location by hand or you could transfer your data over a network. The first approach is inconvenient and, if your name is not Rube Goldberg, impossible to automate, while the second approach can be limited by the quality of your network connection. What you end up using will depend on the specific needs and constraints you're working with.

The fact that most organizational operations require frequent data backups to be useful—and by "frequent" I mean closer to "every hour" than "every week"—means that a system involving cycling through layers of backup media that are physically moved to and forth between your main site and a remote location multiple times a week would be complicated and expensive to implement.

This means in most cases you'll be looking at some kind of network transfer. How good an idea that will be will depend on some practical factors. If your connection to the Internet is capped at a maximum of, say, 50 MB/second, and you've got a terabyte of data that needs to move each day, you should be able to easily see the problem: each transfer will take you nearly two days to complete. That's assuming no one else at your location is using the Internet for anything serious over that time.

Your choices include investing in a faster Internet connection or cutting down on the size of your backups. One way to do that without compromising on the quality of the backup itself is by implementing a system of differential or incremental backups, which we'll discuss a bit later.

Where should your network-transferred archives live? These days, that'll nearly always be in the public cloud. The "cloud," if you're not already acquainted, is made up of the resources of many thousands of public-facing servers and storage devices. The companies that own those resources make it possible for users like us to rent exactly enough space or compute power for our needs. If, for instance, I'll need to run a website that can handle 100,000 visitors a day, but only for the first two days of each month; I can rent just that capacity and only for those days. Similarly, I could push a backup archive to a cloud storage provider where it will remain for as long as I need it or even, after a set time, be automatically moved to a lower-cost, longer-term storage tier. The ability to request instant access to capacity on-demand and in precisely the volume you're using can make many otherwise complex operations simple and cost-effective.

For the kind of backups we're talking about, you'll typically be looking at cloud service providers like Amazon Web Services' (AWS) Simple Storage Service (S3) or, for more limited cases, Dropbox. If you're interested in learning more about the cloud and, in particular the AWS version, my Wiley/Sybex book *AWS Certified Cloud Practitioner Study Guide* (written with my co-author Ben Piper) should give you a lot of food for thought.

Testing Your Backups

Think how much fun you'll have when you suffer a catastrophic data loss and proudly roll out your backup archives only to realize that the data you're expecting just isn't there. Digging into your logs might reveal a problem with the initial backup configuration or that some network failure occurred in the middle. But all that matters right now is that you're sitting on some expensive hardware without the data it needs to make everything work. There's no fixing that one. But it's certainly possible to prevent it happening in the first place. It won't be easy, mind you: there's no simple automated solution I'm aware of. But here's how all the parts of a full test protocol might look:

1. Create a hardware environment that mirrors as closely as possible the production environment you're testing for. You don't need to match the storage and compute capacity, but it will have to run exactly the same OS and software packages and versions. To keep costs down, you might want to build this test environment out of virtual machines.

2. Immediately after creating a new backup archive, copy it to your test environment and put it through the exact same restore process you'd use for the real thing.

3. Finally, test the software itself to make sure everything functions as it should.

4. Repeat for each subsequent backup iteration.

If you have the time and energy, this process could actually be fully automated, with scripts moving archive files between virtual machines and even reporting on automated functionality tests. Whether you want to go that route will depend on your budget and the overall complexity of the environment, but it's something to consider.

Meeting Regulatory Compliance

Regulatory compliance and IT security best practices are largely overlapping. In other words, the government agencies or industry standards groups share most of their goals with the sysadmin running your organization's infrastructure: protecting you, your users, and your customers from attack. So, in most cases at least, you should think of your regulatory requirements as opportunities to improve the stability and value of your operations rather than as a bureaucratic burden (although I certainly won't claim that *all* regulatory requirements are helpful and reasonable).

Thus, when workloads running in the health industry within the United States find themselves subject to the standards of the Health Insurance Portability and Accountability Act (HIPAA) or when companies processing credit card transactions are told by their banks to conform to the Payment Card Industry Data Security Standard (PCI-DSS), there's probably a lot of useful stuff to learn.

One of the elements of most, if not all, regulatory standards involves data retention. If you're working with the health records of tens of thousands of patients, for example, you had better be absolutely certain that those records don't end up leaked or, nearly as bad, lost. So it makes sense to pay close attention to the ways the agencies standing behind HIPAA and PCI-DSS and others expect you to manage your backups. Not only will following their expectations allow you to function in those markets, but they'll also make you a better administrator.

Backup Types

Diving too deeply into the complex world of data backups might divert us a bit too far off topic. But we should at least briefly see some of the main top-level backup strategies. The simplest and most obvious approach is a full backup where you throw everything into the pot each time. As you've seen, this will take so much time and require so much available storage space that it's often impossible. But even here you've got choices. You don't necessarily need to exclude some data just because it won't fit within your available backup space. Instead, you can use one of the methods described in the next sections to update only those resources that have changed or been updated since the most recent backup. As long as you've got a reliable system that'll make sure you're not missing anything, this can simplify and streamline your backups.

Incremental Backups

Incremental backups begin with a single full backup, but, as that happens, the backup software is also recording the state of every object in the archive. Subsequently, when the first *incremental* backup is launched, the source system is scanned for any changes, and only an object that was updated since the first backup or a new object that was created will be part of the increment that's backed up. This second backup will, therefore, be much smaller and complete far more quickly than the original, but a valid and current mirror of the original system will now exist.

A long-term incremental backup protocol might work by doing a full backup on Monday, followed by incremental backups for each of the remaining days of the week. A second complete backup might be performed on the next Monday with the original backup— including all of its increments—"rotated down" to act as a second-tier backup. You might want to maintain a steady rotation of three or four backup cycles before permanently deleting the oldest version.

Increments allow you to significantly cut down on the network and bandwidth needed for backups that still manage to cover everything that needs covering. Should you need to restore your system from a backup archive, you would need access to the original plus all the increments. You will obviously not be managing these steps manually, but, instead, you'll work with backup scripts using tools like Rsync for Linux.

Differential Backups

A differential backup works a lot like its incremental cousin, but, instead of only grabbing object changed since the previous increment, a differential backup will copy and back up *all* the objects changed since *the original full backup*, even if that means a particular file might be copied multiple times in a single cycle. The benefit of differential backups over incremental is that restoring an archive is both faster and easier, since you only need to unpack the initial and most recent archives to be sure you're getting everything. On the other hand, differential backups will often consume more resources as update archives are generated.

Backup Life Cycles

Even when data retention is regulated by law or industry standard, you won't want to keep old archives indefinitely. But I'll bet that you also won't want to have to think about manually deleting old data collections years after they were last used. As you should expect, it's possible to automate the process of administrating archive life cycles.

The AWS S3 service, for instance, allows you to create life-cycle rules that could maintain an archive within the most expensive storage class for, say, a full year; move it to a reduced-access, less expensive storage class for four years; and then, after five full years, delete the archive altogether. This way, you can enjoy the lowest possible costs along with an appropriate access to your data without having to worry about losing track of changes.

As usual, automation is your best friend.

Multitier Backups

Maintaining reliable backup archives for use when life throws a nasty surprise at you is great. But, depending on the way you use your data, it still might not be enough. Consider how the day or two it can take to restore your data from its current setup might be just too long for your organization's needs. Or what if the data you manage happens to be powering operations for a police force or military? The threats facing such infrastructure will probably be strong enough to require extraordinary protection.

Since there's no place yet created that can provide *absolute* security for your backups, your next best option is to leverage the value of more than one storage location, providing a kind of defense in depth. This can take the form of simply replicating backup archives across more than one site, taking advantage of a cloud provider's geographically separated facilities, or maintaining parallel archives using entirely separate cloud storage platforms. The pattern you choose for your archive storage can also be defined by the specific recovery strategy you use. All of these topics will be briefly explored through the rest of this chapter.

Multisite Storage Solutions

When it comes to storage, two sites are definitely better than one. Two separate backup media devices are statistically much less likely to fail over a given time period than one. Two buildings are statistically much less likely to burn down than one. And two countries are statistically much less likely to suffer significant political disruption than one. So it's in your interest to spread your redundant backups as far apart as possible. You might even consider using two distinct software platforms to protect yourself from exposure to a serious bug—anything to avoid facing a single point of failure.

The large global cloud providers like AWS or Microsoft Azure are particularly well positioned in this respect. AWS, for instance, spreads their resources across 20 or so geographic regions, with at least two separate facilities known as *availability zones* (AZs) in each region. A multi-AZ storage class is built by design to ensure that your data is never kept in only one location.

If that kind of replication isn't good enough for you, you can also use third-party orchestration tools to automate the replication of your archives across the resources of *multiple clouds*. This could protect you against vendor lock-in or the possibility of a provider simply going out of business. The approach you choose will reflect your organization's business needs and tolerance for failure.

Disaster Recovery Planning

Your ability to quickly recover from an outage will depend on where your backups are currently kept and, just as important, in what format they're stored. Ideally, you'd like legitimate requests against your application to be redirected to a replacement environment without the need for manual intervention. This process is called *failover* and can be implemented in a way that's effectively invisible to users.

Failover can be automated through the use of one or a combination of Domain Name System (DNS) routing policies, network load balancers, and firewall rules. But it will require the existence of some kind of standby resource stack. That could take the form of a script that launches new servers and populates them with data from your backup archive. Or, for even faster responses, you could invest in a permanent set of prebuilt and regularly updated server resources that mirror the current contents of your "live" servers. Should failover be necessary, those backup servers could be called into active service in seconds.

Such ongoing backup preparedness comes in three flavors.

- *Cold backup stacks* will have replacement server resources available at all times but will require they're populated with software and data before they can be launched.

- *Warm backup stacks* might be kept running permanently with your core application data but will need the latest data imported before they can be launched.

- *Hot backup stacks* are near-perfect mirrors of your production servers and require only request redirection to be brought into service. This, obviously, is the quickest—and most expensive—option.

Fast provisioning of backup resources is something large cloud platforms do particularly well. This alone can be a powerful argument for switching resources to the cloud from your local server rooms, or at least creating some kind of hybrid, cloud-local combination.

Configuring Monitoring and Alerts

System visibility: the more you get of it, the better. Even the smallest computers are mighty complicated things, with millions of lines of code defining how their operating systems, network services, and applications behave. And since nearly all devices these days enjoy full-time network connectivity, changes to their systems are going to happen far more often than in years past. So, to have an idea of how secure you are, you'll definitely want to have a comprehensive and current view of your system's state.

In this chapter, we'll learn about two parallel approaches to helping you see deep inside your box: identifying and catching worrying trends before they present actual trouble and identifying and cutting off existing trouble as quickly as possible to prevent further damage. Those two approaches make use of two tool categories: system logs and intrusion detection tools.

Working with System Logs

The first thing that comes to mind whenever I think about system logs is *information overload*. Digital systems make an awful lot of digital noise, and most of that noise takes the form of unfiltered log files. Figure 8.1 shows a tiny snippet from the log output generated by a typical Linux machine. Since ignoring the whole thing isn't really a solution, the first job of a useful logging system is to give us ways to make sense of the mess.

FIGURE 8.1   Some output from the dmesg command on a Linux Ubuntu 18.04 system. Exciting reading, isn't it?

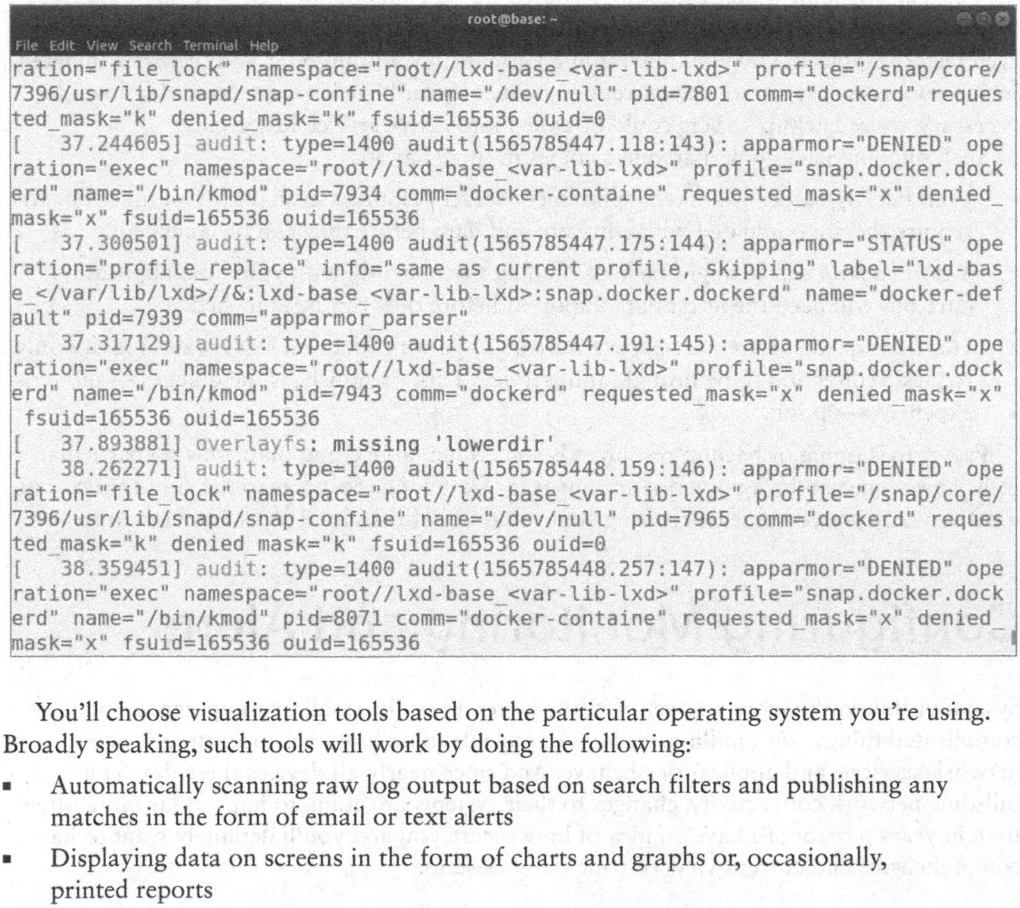

You'll choose visualization tools based on the particular operating system you're using. Broadly speaking, such tools will work by doing the following:

- Automatically scanning raw log output based on search filters and publishing any matches in the form of email or text alerts
- Displaying data on screens in the form of charts and graphs or, occasionally, printed reports

Whichever approach you take, you'll get value out of a system only if there's actually someone at the end of the line watching and capable of responding. To this end, your monitoring system should be simple enough that your administrators will need only a quick glance to recognize signs of trouble, but it should be configured intelligently enough so that you're not getting so many false positives that, eventually, everything is ignored. Expect to spend some time at the beginning fine-tuning your configuration.

Logs can also be used after an attack as part of your forensic analysis. Even if an attack target can no longer be successfully booted (and its logs weren't automatically saved to an external collection system), you can usually still mount the drive using a Linux live boot session and access the logs. Once in, you can examine system log files, focusing on events occurring within the time frame of the attack.

Bear in mind that the data on *encrypted* drives can be accessed only through live boot sessions if you know the decryption key/passphrase.

Intrusion Detection

An effective way to actively monitor your system is by installing some kind of intrusion detection system (IDS). An IDS will regularly run scripts to compare the *actual* state of system resources to their *expected* state. Should unexpected changes to key system configuration files or network behavior be detected, an alert will be issued. IDSs come in two flavors: host-based intrusion detection systems (HIDSs) and network intrusion detection systems (NIDS).

HIDSs track changes to key filesystem configuration files. On a Linux machine, that might mean scanning the file size and change dates of system configuration files in the /etc/ directory hierarchy. You may, for example, get an alert each time an edit of the /etc/passwd file is detected. If the change fits your normal usage pattern (perhaps you recently added a new user account), then you can safely ignore the warning. But if you can't think of any reason for that edit, then you can investigate further. HIDS systems running on Windows machines might focus on changes to the Windows Registry.

NIDSs, on the other hand, analyze records of incoming network traffic. NIDSs are capable of detecting suspicious traffic patterns.

Summary

Reliable backup and recovery plans share an important goal: ensuring that your data and applications will be available to your users as reliably as possible.

It's important to try to visualize all the possible disasters that could hit our organization so you can properly prepare for them. These include hardware failure, theft through hacking, physical disasters like fires, and political disruption.

Where you store your backups—particularly choosing between on-site and cloud solutions—will partly depend on how much data you have and how much network bandwidth you have available to you.

Cloud storage providers like AWS S3 offer cost-effective large-scale storage solutions in multiple tiers that vary in cost, redundancy, and retrieval times.

A backup archive that hasn't been tested for usability should be assumed to be worthless.

Data backup policies must meet any regulatory and industry compliance standards for data retention and protection to which you and your organization are subject.

A backup life cycle defines how long data archives should be maintained at a particular level of accessibility and when, if ever, they should be destroyed.

System behavior should be constantly monitored for suspicious behavior through log data visualization tools and some kind of intrusion detection system.

Exam Essentials

Understand what constitutes a full and usable backup.   For a backup to be useful, it must include all the data you'll need to quickly restore your applications to a working state.

Understand the kinds of problems that can render a backup unusable.   Backup media can fail, backup contents can prove deficient, and archives can be out-of-date.

Understand the key considerations for building a disaster recovery plan.   The recovery point objective (RPO) represents the maximum amount of data you could lose without destabilizing your organization. The recovery time objective (RTO) is the maximum amount of time you can survive before your application must return to a functional state.

Understand the importance of redundancy for your backups.   Concentrating your backup archives in a single location or using a single software platform can expose it to a "single point of failure," reducing its chances of survival.

Understand various backup strategies.   A differential backup saves all changed objects with each backup action subsequent to the most recent *full* backup. Incremental backups save only those objects changed since the most recent *incremental* backup.

Understand various backup patterns.   Failover is the ability of a system to reroute incoming requests to a standby resource stack if the production stack has failed. You can use cold, warm, and hot backup stacks for failovers, depending on how critical immediate recovery is to your organization.

Review Questions

1. What is the greatest risk associated with ransomware attacks?
   A. The theft of the identities of your system administrators
   B. The effective destruction of your physical servers
   C. The catastrophic loss of access to your own data
   D. The theft of the rightful ownership of your third-party software licenses

2. Under normal circumstances where it's important to keep archive size down, what elements should a full system backup include?
   A. System configuration, application, log, account, and user data
   B. Application and user data
   C. System configuration, hardware profile, application, and user data
   D. Complete snapshot images that include virtual filesystems

3. What best describes a recovery point objective (RPO)?
   A. The worst-case scenario you can anticipate impacting your application availability
   B. The system state required by your organization to meet its minimum requirements
   C. The maximum length of time your organization could afford to be without an unavailable application
   D. The ideal functioning state of your organization's application

4. What best describes a recovery time objective (RTO)?
   A. The system state required by your organization to meet its minimum requirements
   B. The worst-case scenario you can anticipate impacting your application availability
   C. The ideal functioning state of your organization's application
   D. The maximum length of time your organization could afford to be without an unavailable application

5. Why should you back up your data to multiple storage media formats?
   A. Because any one media device could degrade and fail
   B. Because the location where you store your data could be damaged by fire, etc.
   C. Because compatible hardware for any one media device could become impossible to find
   D. Because live application data quickly becomes outdated

6. What consideration could make it difficult for you to regularly push your large data backups to the cloud?
   A. Limited available network bandwidth
   B. The inferior reliability of cloud storage option
   C. The security of your data during transit
   D. The risk of losing your backed up data altogether

7. Why should you want to ensure that your systems and data meet regulatory compliance standards? (Choose two.)

- **A.** Because regulatory compliance will almost always be more cost effective
- **B.** Because many elements of regulatory compliance standards are important for maintaining the integrity of your data
- **C.** Because complying with standards allows you to work within controlled industries
- **D.** Because most enterprise software is designed to fail when running noncompliant workloads

8. What will accurately describe a differential backup?

- **A.** All objects within a target storage device will be backed up.
- **B.** Only objects that have changed or been added since the last full backup operation will be backed up.
- **C.** Objects will be backed up according to a randomly generated schedule, calibrated to ensure that, over time, all objects are copied.
- **D.** Only objects that have changed or been added since the most recent backup operation will be backed up.

9. What will accurately describe an incremental data backup?

- **A.** Only objects that have changed or been added since the most recent backup operation will be backed up.
- **B.** Only objects that have changed or been added since the last full backup operation will be backed up.
- **C.** All objects within a target storage device will be backed up.
- **D.** Objects will be backed up according to a randomly generated schedule, calibrated to ensure that, over time, all objects are copied.

10. What considerations might force you to elect to configure incremental rather than differential backups?

- **A.** The learning curve necessary to configure successful differential backups
- **B.** The existence of sensitive and private data
- **C.** The existence of data spread across multiple remote sites
- **D.** Limits to your available network bandwidth and storage capacity

11. Which of the following are effective ways to diversify the architecture of your backups? (Choose three.)

- **A.** Store archives using multiple software systems.
- **B.** Store archives using multiple hardware device platforms.
- **C.** Store archives using multiple version increments.
- **D.** Store archives across multiple geographic regions.

12. What is it about their platform architecture that allows large cloud providers to better protect you against major physical outages?

    A. Widely distributed physical infrastructure

    B. Strong firewall protection

    C. The ability to scale resources up and down quickly

    D. Large, well-trained teams of engineers

13. What would you call an emergency recovery system that maintains up-to-date copies of your application data running at all times?

    A. A load balancer

    B. A cold backup

    C. A warm backup

    D. A hot backup

14. Which of the following monitoring systems can be configured to actively look for signs that your server's filesystem has been tampered with?

    A. Host-based intrusion detection systems (HIDSs)

    B. JournalD (Linux systems)

    C. The `dmesg` facility (Linux systems)

    D. Network intrusion detection systems (NIDSs)

15. How can monitoring data be effectively visualized in a format that's easy to consume? (Choose two.)

    A. By automating the filtering of log data for "interesting" entries that are forwarded to administrators for visualization

    B. By using visualization software that can display log data using charts and graphs

    C. By scheduling times for careful manual reviews of full log files

    D. By streaming log data in a background window on every admin's desktop

16. Which system resource can be used to help you understand system vulnerabilities before, during, and after an attack?

    A. Intrusion detection systems

    B. Network intrusion detection systems

    C. Logs

    D. VPNs

Chapter

9

Resource Isolation Design Patterns

THE LPI SECURITY ESSENTIALS EXAM TOPICS COVERED IN THIS CHAPTER INCLUDE THE FOLLOWING:

✓ **021.2 Risk assessment and management**

- Awareness of Information Security Management Systems (ISMS) and Information Security Incident Response Plans and Teams

✓ **024.1 Networks, network services and the Internet**

- Understanding of the concepts of routing and Internet Service Providers (ISPs)

- Understanding of the concepts of IP networks and the Internet

Resource Isolation

Design Patt

Think for a moment about the way they build big ships. Multiple watertight compartments divided by (vertical) bulkheads and (horizontal) decks can protect a ship from sinking in the event the outer hull is compromised. The idea is that even if damage to the ship causes leaks, water accumulation can be limited to only the compartments closest to the trouble. The remaining compartments can continue to provide buoyancy.

That's a nice way to think about IT security. Given that you're almost certainly going to be the target of many malicious attacks over time, and given that some of those attacks are bound to have at least some success, it makes sense to try to limit the damage they cause. Building digital equivalents of bulkheads and decks into your infrastructure design can make a big difference.

By "design" here, I mean more than just the way you might write software or configure your IT resource stacks—although I definitely mean those, too. But beyond that, I want to encourage you to think in terms of isolation in the context of all your interactions with digital devices.

Take your smartphone, for instance. Or, more to the point: what's going to happen when someone *else* takes your smartphone? How much of your important data will that thief now possess? What important accounts will he now have access to? Will you be able to authenticate to existing MFA-enabled accounts? Are you sure you'll be able to realize you've been robbed and find a computer where you can log into all those accounts and update their authentication before your online and financial and legal identity is no longer yours?

Why not protect yourself up front by putting some distance—a virtual watertight bulkhead—between your accounts and the attacker? One obvious step is to password protect and encrypt your mobile devices. Another could be to use a disposable email account for all the services you access from your phone. That way, if you are hit, the main account you use for serious logins like banking and work will still be under your control and you'll only need to choose a new throwaway email account to replace access to the stuff you use when you're on the road. Forwarding emails from your main account to the one associated with your phone lets you keep up-to-date on your personal and business lives without unnecessary risk.

This *account isolation* principle could also apply to any digital assistants you use. No one really knows how much data is being collected by tools like Amazon's Alexa, Apple's Siri, or Google Assistant or what they're doing with it. Nor do we really know how exposed that data is to the risk of third-party theft. So it might make sense to avoid associating your assistant with your primary email address and personal identity accounts—just to limit your damage in the event of a security incident.

Those are some ways to apply *isolation* to your personal online activity. The rest of the chapter will look at how it can be used as part of larger IT systems. We'll look at designing networks, creating "safe-space" sandbox environments, and building virtual walls to more closely control who gets access to specific resources.

Configuring Network Firewalling

In Chapter 3, "Controlling Access to Your Assets," you learned how network traffic is controlled and directed by physical or software firewalls and routers. But the level of control that's possible using those devices can also allow you to effectively segment your resources into distinct and isolated partitions. You could configure relatively open access to one group of devices, while protecting other, more sensitive operations behind more restrictive controls.

For cloud providers like AWS, you can use virtual resource organization tools like a virtual private cloud (VPC) or a security group to provide a similar functionality. For local infrastructure it's common, in addition, to divide your assets into separate physical networks, using cabling or wireless configuration to build the "walls" that keep your networks from overlapping.

Here are a few scenarios that make use of this kind of isolation pattern.

Balancing Public and Private Networks

A common approach to building multitiered web applications is to place your web servers in a public-facing network, while leaving the database servers that feed the web servers their data in a private network that restricts access to only those admins and services that need it. Figure 9.1 illustrates what that kind of setup might look like. The principle? Protect what you can and expose only what you must.

FIGURE 9.1   Public-facing web servers are allowed fairly open access from public networks, while backend database servers are far better protected.

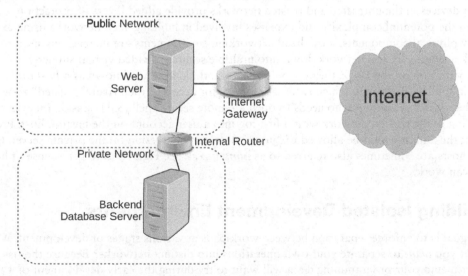

For even tighter access protection, you can create a third network, often called a DMZ (an acronym borrowed from the geopolitical term *demilitarized zone*). The DMZ serves as a safety valve between the "untrusted" public network, where resources like your web servers can live, and the private, "trusted" network for your local infrastructure. A typical DMZ architecture, as shown in Figure 9.2, would place your local resources within a network behind a very restrictive firewall, public-facing resources served by a separate network router "beyond" that first firewall, and then a second firewall beyond the public network.

FIGURE 9.2   A common dual-firewall DMZ setup

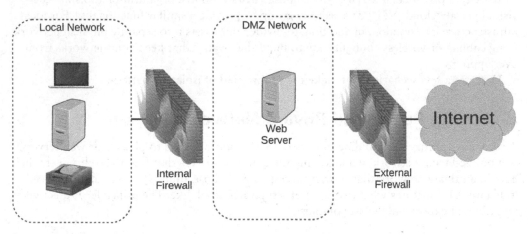

The extra network configurations and authentication needed to create connections between devices in the untrusted and trusted networks provide added layers of protection. Given the potential complexity and expenses involved in building such networks using exclusively physical components, virtualized networking environments are increasingly used to break a single physical network down into multiple securely divided virtual subnets.

A variation on the DMZ theme would use a stand-alone server known as a *bastion host* within the DMZ through which external requests for access to the private "trusted" zone can be routed. An admin who needs to open a remote secure shell (SSH) session on a server running in the trusted network would first log into a user account on the bastion host. From there, the admin would be allowed to "jump" onto an SSH session on the private server. Bastion hosts are sometimes also referred to as *jump boxes*. See Figure 9.3 to get a sense of how this can work.

Building Isolated Development Environments

The goal is to enforce separation between workloads at various stages of development. Why might you *want* to separate your own operations into distinct networks? Because the risky experiments your programming team will want to try during the early development of a product could easily escape the lab and impact any servers running on the network. You

FIGURE 9.3   A bastion host is a server placed within a DMZ through which remote admins can access resources in a private network.

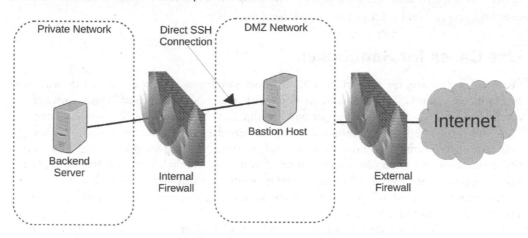

want your developers to be able to innovate and experiment, but you also want to protect your production resources from any monsters the developers might accidentally let loose.

Organizations will often carve three environments out of their overall infrastructure. One environment—using a private network—might be for the early development of future versions of their applications. A second environment could be dedicated to deploying a final pre-publication version. This "staging" environment, as it's known, is used to test a new software release on a technology stack that's pretty much identical to what it will use once it's published. This provides one last opportunity to confirm that everything is working as it should. The third environment is for production, and it's where the release version that'll be consumed by your users will stay for its active life.

What all three environments have in common is that they do *not* share a single network or server assets. The system works because you maintain close control over the context within which each version of your software runs. If something ever does go wrong, you should always be able to rule out cross-environment contamination as a cause. And you should also be confident that at no point will you ever face an unnecessary security risk.

For local infrastructure, isolated development environments are built using traditional physical or virtual networking. Cloud providers offer simpler—and often much cheaper—alternatives for isolation using, as in the case of AWS, distinct VPCs or even organizational accounts for each environment you need.

Working with Sandbox Environments

Do you or the developers and admins you love sometimes need to test new technologies? Regularly learning to use new tools is a necessary component of many technology careers, but making mistakes with unfamiliar configuration settings can be a threat to the stability, or even security, of your work computers. The perfect place where you can play with all the new toys you can find is known as a *sandbox*.

Use Cases for Sandboxes

From my experience, the truly magical thing about sandboxes is how quickly I can provision and launch a *clean* OS environment. Working with a "previously enjoyed" system always carries the risk that the results you get will be influenced by something you—or someone else—did earlier. Perhaps you installed some software dependency that won't automatically exist elsewhere, or maybe there's a system configuration allowing (or preventing) a connection to a remote resource you forgot you set. If you want to reliably test a software application, you really need complete control of the base environment you're using. For that, there's no substitute for a fresh OS with a completely predictable software and networking stack. For *that*, there's nothing like a sandbox.

Using virtualization technologies like Docker (`www.docker.com`) and LXD (`https://linuxcontainers.org/lxd`) containers, or virtual machines via Oracle's VirtualBox (`www.virtualbox.org`), I can quite literally tell myself "It would sure be nice to try that tool" and, within 60 seconds, have an appropriately isolated, pristine, sandboxed Linux OS running at my fingertips. Of course, you're not restricted to *unaltered* OS environments. You can just as easily create a custom image of an OS—say, Ubuntu Linux with WordPress preinstalled—and use that image as the base for any number of sandboxes.

So sandboxes can be great for building quick and easy workspaces to fit whatever testing needs come your way. But, at the same time, as we noted, they're also useful for protecting your nonsandbox resources. This is nowhere more obvious than when you're engaged in forensic analysis.

Forensic analysis, if you haven't yet had the pleasure, is the process of analyzing a digital device that's been subject to an attack using, for instance, dangerous malware. The trick is to access the malware and learn about its origins, operational capacity, and vulnerabilities without taking a chance on compromising your own infrastructure. Practically, that means you don't want the infection breaking out and spreading to your healthy devices.

In this context, your sandbox could consist of a stand-alone PC lacking any network connectivity. Such a setup is commonly called *air gapping* because there is no physical Ethernet (or wireless) connection between the computer and a network and, therefore, no possible escape or communication route for the malware. Under such circumstances it can be possible to safely engage in your analysis.

Sandbox Designs

Besides the air gap sandboxes we just discussed, which are fairly straightforward to implement, isolated environments also come in some other equally yummy flavors. When it comes to building complex multiserver environments, looking for simplicity and cost savings will often lead you to virtualization.

Hypervisor virtualization involves a host server whose compute, storage, and networking resources can be partitioned into multiple virtual servers, each happily running without the slightest clue that it's not completely in charge of an entire machine. When properly configured, one virtual machine (VM) should, unless you explicitly permit it, have no access to the data or resources of any other VM running on the same hypervisor.

This flexibility and isolation can make VMs an excellent tool for building sandboxes. But many hypervisor platforms, including Xen and KVM, can be notoriously difficult to install and provision. Oracle's VirtualBox is a *hosted hypervisor* that installs on any OS like any other application, but that gives you a highly configurable environment for running your Linux or Windows VMs. As you can see from Figure 9.4, the VirtualBox Settings dialog gives you a high level of control over the way your VM will operate, including exactly what its network neighborhood will look like. This lets you define exactly the connectivity and usability options you need.

FIGURE 9.4   The VirtualBox network adapter configuration dialog

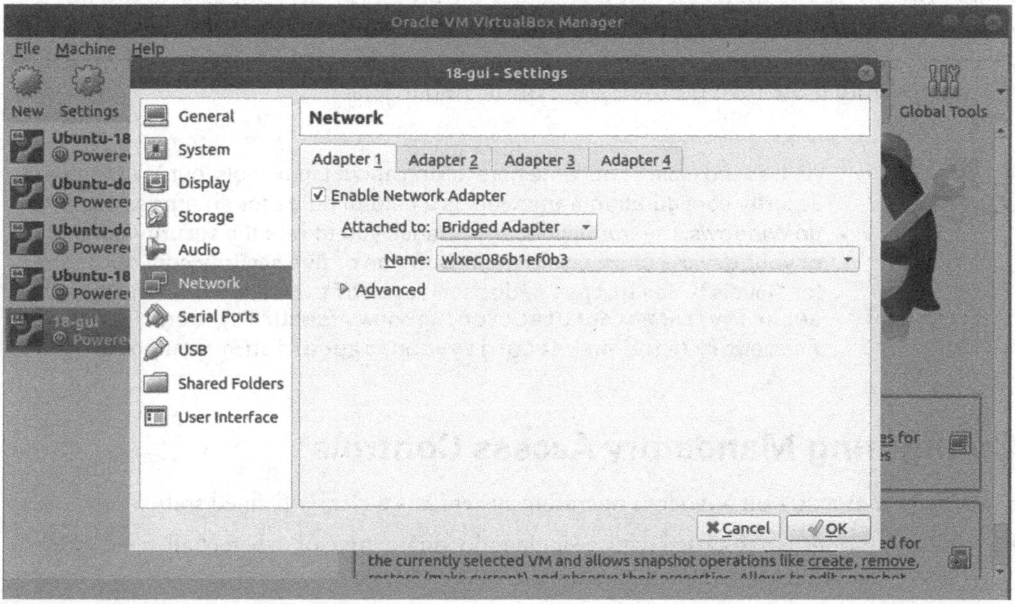

Lightweight container technologies like Docker and LXD, unlike hypervisors, will share not only hardware resources but also the host operating system's software kernel. This architecture is responsible for much of the superior speed and performance you'll get from containers, but, assuming you've configured things properly, you shouldn't lose any isolation. The most obvious downside to containers is that they're not meant to provide virtual platforms using graphic interfaces. As long as you're only after a terminal login connection, you should consider containers for your sandbox.

Just as you saw earlier with development/production environments, you can create secure and effective sandboxes using cloud infrastructure elements like Amazon's VPCs. Just realize that you'll probably need to do a good job tightening up the security group rules to achieve the level of isolation you need.

Controlling Local System Access

Having discussed isolating your data and resources within larger networks, how about spending some time talking about protecting resources belonging on one user from other users within a single computer? You really do want to have this conversation. After all, it all makes sense as part of those watertight bulkheads we met with earlier. Think of this kind of protection as the final dry compartment within a very wet ship.

How you create access controls will depend on your particular OS—or the particular cloud provider you're using, for that matter. But the process always begins with the way your users establish their identities, which usually works through login accounts. Once a user account is established, you'll be able to use your system's tools to ensure that no one manages to grab more than their fair share of the resource pie.

We'll spend most of our time here talking about Linux tools, but Microsoft's security configuration framework is a helpful guide for enterprise security on Windows. The framework encourages you to rate the security needs of your devices to associate them with one or five security configurations (or "levels"). See https://docs.microsoft.com/en-us/windows/security/threat-protection/windows-security-configuration-framework/windows-security-configuration-framework.

Configuring Mandatory Access Controls

Everything that exists on a modern operating system has a clearly defined status.

- A user account is associated with a single individual who can, when challenged, present the correct authentication information.

- A running process is associated with one particular user account or group and no other.

- An object—like a file, directory, or network port—is accessible to running processes according to the permissions associated with the user or group that owns (or *launched*) the process.

Thus, if you initiate a process to, say, create, edit, and save a new text file, the system will permit the process to complete successfully only if it involves access to appropriate objects. That, in this case, would mean you're trying to create your file in a directory on the filesystem for which your user account has rights.

One example of such a system is the way Linux assigns permissions to *users*, *groups*, and *others* to control their ability to read, write, and execute objects. This kind of system is known as *discretionary access control* (DAC). It's "discretionary" because certain users can choose to invoke administration powers and execute operations beyond the normal scope given their account.

However, in many scenarios, DAC controls aren't secure enough. For such cases there are systems that enforce stricter policies known as *mandatory access control* (MAC). MAC policies on multiuser systems are usually set by a single central admin and are meant to be difficult or impossible to override even for users with some administration powers (like *sudo* users on Linux).

One common implementation of a MAC is Security-Enhanced Linux (SELinux), which is widely used on Red Hat Enterprise Linux-related distributions. SELinux policies can be used at the kernel level to protect the most vulnerable resources from unauthorized access and use.

It should be noted that false positives can be common on systems where SELinux is active. A user might try to install a new software package and discover that the default SELinux rules are getting in the way. Frustrated by the complications inherent in SELinux configurations, users with top-level admin access will often just disable SELinux altogether, promising themselves that they'll "figure everything out and restart it sometime later." It's worth remembering that "sometime later" will probably never arrive, and your system will remain vulnerable indefinitely. Just saying.

Other important MAC systems include Ubuntu's Apparmor—which, by reputation, is significantly easier to use than SELinux—and Mandatory Integrity Control (MIC) for Windows. MIC works by rating the trustworthiness—or *Integrity Level* (IL)—of a user or group (as defined by its access token) and deciding whether that IL is high enough to permit access to an object based on the object's security descriptor.

Setting Usage Quotas

No matter how fast PC memory and compute power grow and how cheap mass storage gets, there will always be limits to how much is available. So from time to time, the many processes running concurrently on your computer might fight over access to one resource or another. Sometimes it'll be an illegitimate process—like an unauthorized cryptomining operation—that's trying to grab all the goodies for itself. To protect your system from being overwhelmed and crippled by a rogue process, it's wise to set limits—or quotas—to how much of a particular resource a particular user or process can request.

Linux uses the quota tool to control the amount of disk space each user or group can use. The more modern *control groups* (commonly known as *cgroups*) can be used to apply limits to how much memory, CPU utilization, and disk I/O throughput a process may consume. Windows has its own Quota tools.

Cloud platforms also provide tools for capping usage. In fact, most AWS services have built-in default limits on how much is available to be consumed by any one account.

Summary

Carefully consider how you use mobile devices and smart digital assistants to ensure your data and identity aren't facing more risk than you can justify.

Intelligently dividing your network into smaller segments can reduce your exposure to risk.

Virtualization tools like VirtualBox and Docker containers are well-suited for creating clean and isolated environments for running more secure workloads.

The way users consume system resources can be limited by tools like Quota and cgroups. Such limits can prevent rogue and unauthorized processes from dominating and, eventually, compromising overall system integrity.

Exam Essentials

Understand how you can use network isolation to protect valuable infrastructure resources.   Firewalls and other network configuration tools can be used to segment your resources, reducing risk exposure for vulnerable devices.

Be familiar with common network architectures that can improve infrastructure security.   Multitiered network designs can provide significant protection. Such designs include DMZs, bastion hosts, and networks divided by purpose (development/staging/production).

Understand how building clean and isolated "sandboxed" environments can provide more secure operations.   The risks to your operations associated with testing or learning new technologies can be greatly reduced by partitioning isolated environments for your early development exercises.

Understand how OS operations can gain additional security through the use of mandatory access control (MAC).   SELinux and Apparmor on Linux, and Mandatory Integrity Control for Windows, are examples of MACs that can be configured to set absolute limits on access to system resources. Quota for Windows and cgroups for Linux are tools for limiting the consumption of resources.

Review Questions

1. What is "resource isolation?"

    A. Closely monitoring infrastructure activity and breaking down log output by resource

    B. Controlling access between infrastructure elements to limit the scope of damage caused by an attack

    C. Deploying resources across multiple physical sites to increase high availability

    D. Deploying as few resources as necessary to reduce your vulnerability surface

2. Which network design models are primarily intended to increase the security of private networked resources? (Choose two.)

    A. DMZ

    B. Multiavailability zone

    C. Production/staging/development networks

    D. Bastion host

3. What tools exist to isolate network segments and the resources they host from each other? (Choose two.)

    A. Virtual networking environments (like VPCs on AWS)

    B. Firewall devices

    C. Auto scaling software

    D. Failover routing rules

4. What best explains the origin of the computing term *sandboxing*?

    A. A sandbox promises an enjoyable experience—something made possible for compute environments.

    B. Any "box" is intended to reliably hold multiple, nominally related objects.

    C. Computer circuitry is often built on a silicon (sand) surface.

    D. A traditional sandbox is a safe and clean play area where children can learn new skills—goals also desirable for application development environments.

5. Which technologies are best suited to the quick provisioning of clean and isolated sandboxed compute environments? (Choose two.)

    A. Cloud compute instances

    B. Docker

    C. LXD

    D. VMware vSphere

6. What value can sandboxed environments have for digital forensic analysis? (Choose two.)

    A. Sandboxing makes it possible to rule out the presence of unexpected software installations or configuration in your analysis environment.

    B. Sandboxing makes it easier to prevent the spread of any malware that's infected target systems.

    C. Sandboxing makes it possible to conduct quicker and more efficient analysis.

    D. Sandboxing makes it easy to test performance for separate but comparable systems.

7. Within the context of building compute isolation environments, which of the following features is an advantage of containers over hypervisor technologies?

    A. Superior technical support

    B. Fast provisioning, launching, and performance

    C. The availability of native graphic interfaces

    D. Increased application durability

8. What is the primary value of deploying an "air-gapped" server?

    A. You're provided with optimal wireless network connectivity.

    B. You're provided with optimal wired (ethernet) network connectivity.

    C. You're assured optimal resource isolation.

    D. Air-gapped servers are positioned for safe and controlled network access to multiple environments.

9. What best defines the way a discretionary access control (DAC) system works?

    A. Access controls are absolute and permit no exceptions.

    B. Access controls are flexible and can be overridden by any legitimately authenticated user.

    C. Access controls are flexible and can be overridden only by an administrator user.

    D. Access controls are dependent on context and can only sometimes be overridden by authenticated users.

10. Which of these can be considered a mandatory access control (MAC) system? (Choose two.)

    A. SELinux

    B. Network access control lists (ACLs)

    C. Apparmor

    D. Firewall routing rules

11. What's the simplest and most effective way to protect against cryptomining operations being run through compromised user accounts?

    A. SELinux

    B. ACLs

    C. Usage quotas

    D. Containers

Appendix

Answers to Review Questions

Chapter 1: Using Digital Resources Responsibly

1. B. Falsely and illegally directing law enforcement authorities toward a nonexistent crime is known as swatting. Persistent and unwanted monitoring and harassing of a target is cyberstalking. A coordinated social media–based attack against an individual involving large numbers of attackers is cybermobbing.

2. C. Falsely and illegally directing law enforcement authorities toward a nonexistent crime is known as swatting. Persistent and unwanted monitoring and harassing of a target is cyberstalking. Publicizing a target's personal contact and location information without authorization is doxxing.

3. A, D. Your organization would generally not be liable for what employees do using public or publicly available forums. Having said that, this should not be misconstrued as legal advice. Consult your own legal counsel for practical information.

4. A, C. Old social medial posts and official court records are (usually) meant to reside in the public domain and, hence, should be considered public.

5. C, D. Text messaging is rarely performed within a browser, and a password (should) never be recorded in a readable format by any software.

6. B, C. Should you want to access your personal data (even data stored off-site), there are usually ways to do that. Having to update your information of remote databases might be inconvenient, but it's hardly a consequence of the misuse of your personal data (and hardly a major concern).

7. D. The GDPR mandates the protection, privacy, and safety of personal data moving through EU territories.

8. B. HIPAA, GDPR, and SOX are all mandates originating with governments (either the U.S. government of the European Union).

9. C, D. It's highly unlikely that a privacy policy document would reveal the potential for data abuse or any details of the application design.

10. B. Spoofing (often, though not exclusively) involves misrepresenting the origin address within an email message.

11. C. Phishing involves attempting to trick individuals into revealing private information.

12. A, B. Outbound links have no automatic correlation with content quality. Website encryption can be easily enabled for even fraudulent sites.

Chapter 2: What Are Vulnerabilities and Threats?

1. B, D. While cost savings and application efficiency are important business considerations, they're not particularly important from a security perspective.

2. C. Network firewalls and malware detection tools are designed to control system access, but not primarily to track the origins of processes. Availability is a top-level goal, but it, too, is not primarily concerned with process tracking.

3. A. Holes in your defenses or entities aiming to disable your infrastructure are "threats," not vulnerabilities. Hard-to-replace data is a "target" rather than a vulnerability.

4. B. "Compute devices issued private network IP addresses" and "Multiple simple systems combined as part of the operation of complex environments" describe local network configurations (of using NAT). The IoT is, in fact, networks of mass-produced compute devices that regularly exchange data.

5. B, C. Disrupting network connectivity is not a significant motivation for attacks because it doesn't normally present useful opportunities for causing damage or extracting private data.

6. C, D. Using weak passwords or untrusted websites isn't healthy, but they're not directly related to browsers.

7. B, C. Firewall rules are a solution for software, not physical, vulnerabilities. It's rare for older hardware to be more vulnerable from a security perspective.

8. A, B, D. Online services—like Gmail or Salesforce—are generally maintained and patched by their providers. As a rule, you're responsible only for the software you install and administrate.

9. A, D. Strange behavior from team members represents a possible internal threat, not external. Effective use of business applications is not necessarily a security concern.

10. A, C. USB storage devices and Ethernet cables don't use wireless connections.

11. A. A backdoor is the expression commonly used to describe an undocumented (and, often, unauthorized) method of accessing a compute device.

12. B. Securing third-party network connections and the security status of privately owned devices is beyond the scope of government mandates.

13. A, C, D. While avoiding online e-commerce and banking sites would protect you from data leaks, for most people it's not a practical solution.

14. C. A phishing attack is an attempt to convince the target that they should review personal and private information to unauthorized individuals or data-capture applications.

15. B, D. OSINT gathering is done using publicly available data and does not require physical access. While OSINT methodologies can be used among efforts to combat attacks, they can also be effective as part of criminal activities.

16. C. Ransomware involves inserting malicious software to encrypt local data, requiring payment of a ransom before access is returned to the owner.

17. A, D. There are, at this point at least, no online services useful for preventing ransomware attacks. Giving in to ransomware authors' demands is generally a terrible idea and should never be used as anything but a last resort—with the understanding that you probably won't get your data back anyway.

18. B, D. Distributed denial-of-service attacks take over vulnerable network-connected devices and employ their resources to launch sustained requests for service from a target, preventing it from performing its normal services. Such attacks aren't looking to acquire or destroy valuable data.

19. A, B. ARP spoofing and MAC flooding both attempt to change the way network devices handle traffic in order to compromise network activities. Social engineering in general, and phishing in particular, are methods designed to fool people into revealing private information inappropriately.

20. B. A "zombie" is a compute device whose resources have been hijacked as part of an attack against a third party. This is a common feature of an attack using the combined resources of many IoT devices.

Chapter 3: Controlling Access to Your Assets

1. B. Mitigation is made up of the steps an organization takes to reduce the impact of an attack against your IT infrastructure.

2. C. Shoulder surfers are people, not devices. Keystroke loggers and operating systems are installed on your computer; hence, they're not external.

3. A. Live Linux sessions require no password login because, by default, they create a perfectly clean environment involving no preexisting private data. A live Linux session is no more vulnerable to external attack than any other computer running within a private network. While hidden malware could be delivered along with a live Linux image, it's highly unlikely and would, therefore, not count as a "primary risk."

4. D. You should protect servers and PCs from power surges and interruptions using surge protectors and USB power supplies, but power supplies are not a possible source for spyware. The primary risk facing data stored on portable data volumes or smartphones is of theft, rather than integration of spyware or malware.

5. B. A software firewall can protect your computer from unauthorized network access but won't protect against physical theft. An OS password will prevent an attacker only from loading the OS but won't keep him from accessing the data drive. It's good to control physical access to your computer, but, in this case, it seems, it was stolen anyway.

6. B. The MBR is a small software program stored on the boot drive itself that's used to boot-strap the OS. It's not firmware and assumes the hardware environment information passed to it is correct. The OS kernel is loaded only at a later stage (and is also not firmware). The root partition is a section of a storage drive set as the base of an OS filesystem within which all other directories are kept.

7. A, B, D. Empty spaces would probably not be acceptable as valid characters by most application authentication software and would thus fail.

8. C. Verification is a method for confirming the truth of a claim. Authentication is the process of establishing the identity of a user or role. Neither has any direct connection to authorization. Encryption is a method for changing the visible nature of data to make it impossible to read without access to a decryption key.

9. A. MFA is an authentication method that requires more than one type of information—typically a password and a PIN sent to a preset device.

10. B. Large enterprise operations will normally require commercial firewall appliances. Stand-alone computers are usually well served by built-in, OS-based application firewall software (like Ubuntu's UFW).

11. A, C, D. Routing rules are applied by firewall tools installed at each "hop" along a packet's journey and are not included in the packet header itself.

12. A. Antivirus software is designed to find and disable malware. Firewall rules are used to protect systems from abuse caused by threats—including malware. Spam describes unsolicited mass email messaging.

13. A. Because they can read the payload contents of network packets, layer 7 firewalls can be more accurate. Greater throughput and a wider range of protocols are features of layer 3 firewalls. All firewalls can work with packet source and destination information.

14. C. `Amazon.com` is the hostname used by this website. `https` tells a browser that the protocol used for this page is secure HTTP. `1119490707` points to a specific file or object.

15. D. A protocol of `https`—as opposed to `http`—tells you that the site you're loading is properly encrypted.

16. B, C. If anything, the firewalling tools offered by cloud providers are more powerful and safe than the ones you might use locally. Cloud providers do *not* automatically handle firewalling for your virtual machine instances. That's your responsibility.

17. B, C. HTTPS encryption is, in fact, a very important part of website security. There is, at this point at least, no known flaw that would allow a browser to display HTTPS incorrectly.

18. A, C. The use of a .com (or .org, etc.) domain is no guarantee of the reliability of a download—many criminal organizations have such domains. Unfortunately, there are plenty of malware-infested business productivity packages out there.

19. B, C. While some progress has been made, one can't honestly say that mobile app security is "under control" just yet. Malware is frequently incorporated into productivity apps for mobile—and desktop—systems.

20. C. There is no repo called "SafeStore." Chocolatey is a Windows software manager. Homebrew is for macOS. YUM is a repo for Red Hat and related Linux distributions.

Chapter 4: Controlling Network Connections

1. B. The protocol defining how remote connections can be securely encrypted describes Secure Shell (SSH). The protocol defining how network packets are directed between hosts is the Internet Protocol (IP). The protocol defining a bidirectional interactive text-oriented communication facility describes Telnet.

2. A. Tracking operation owners is important, but it's not the primary purpose of IP addresses. Individual addresses are not necessarily helpful for identifying subnet ranges. IP addresses on their own will not increase (or harm) network efficiency.

3. B, C. No single octet of an IPv4 address can have a value higher than 255, so 10.0.260.10 is invalid. IPv4 addresses must have 4 octets, so 22.198.65/24—with its three octets (and a CIDR value)—is invalid.

4. D. There are approximately four billion possible IP addresses available for the IPv4 network.

5. A. The /24 CIDR netmask value tells us that three of the 8-bit octets (8*3=24) represent the network. That means that the three leftmost octets (192.168.4) would be the correct answer.

6. D. NAT addressing is unlikely to reduce incidents of malicious spoofing or speed network transfers, and it definitely does *not* simplify network configuration administration.

7. A. IPv6 addresses are made up of eight 16-bit octets made up of hexadecimal numbers.

8. B, D. Both options B and D represent the same (valid) address: contiguous octets containing only zeros may be replaced by ::. Option A has only seven octets, and option C has three, rather than two, colons representing the zeros.

9. C. The distribution and use of web addresses is controlled by domain name registrars, not DNS servers. DNS servers translate human-readable URLs into numeric IP addresses so browsers will know where to look for web resources—not the other way around.

10. A. A netmask defines the network portion of an IP address. A subnet is a block of IP addresses defined from a within a larger network. A network domain is a collection of network hosts associated with a single owner. A host is a compute device connected to a network.

11. A, B. All private NAT addresses must fall within one of these three ranges:

    10.0.0.0 to 10.255.255.255
    172.16.0.0 to 172.31.255.255
    192.168.0.0 to 192.168.255.255

12. A, C. Network security audits aren't typically concerned with network connectivity and efficiency.

13. B. The correct switch to restrict an Nmap operation to only the 100 most popular ports is -F (it must be uppercase). Nmap, in this case, also requires full CIDR notation (/24).

14. A, C, D. The process ID would be a value that's relevant only to an operating system and wouldn't be detected or recorded as part of network transfers.

15. B. `wiresharkd` and `wired` don't exist (as scan tools, at any rate). Nmap can be automated, but it's not identical in features with Wireshark.

16. B, C. Bug-free software is nice, but it's not primarily a security consideration. Developers who meet execution deadlines and remain within budget don't exist.

17. A, B, C. Unauthorized and unsecured webcams are a problem but will likely have only a minimal impact on physical security.

18. A, D. The power supply and unauthorized physical access to the facility aren't primarily network vulnerabilities.

19. B, C. Older PCs might run unsupported and unpatched software, but the fact that the hardware itself is old is not, itself, normally a security issue. Older network cabling will be slow but will not present a security threat.

20. D. Even if it might be less common, malware can be written for open-source software just as easily as commercial software. Viruses can indeed also infect Linux systems—especially via web browsers.

Chapter 5: Encrypting Your Data at Rest

1. A. Decryption—the opposite of encryption—involves applying an encryption key to encrypted text to restore it to a readable format.

2. D. Neither asymmetric nor hybrid encryption protocols require the manual sharing of private keys. Duplex encryption doesn't exist.

3. B. Running pure asymmetric encryption sessions can be resource-intensive. There is no need to expose any private keys using these methods. The same algorithms can be used for all modern encryption protocols. Asymmetric encryption will, if anything, require less human intervention than other methods.

4. C. A hash is the encryption of data done in such a way that it can't be decrypted but can be identified as an exact copy of an original. This is widely used for confirming a password as legitimate.

5. A. Encryption won't normally have a noticeable impact on performance or disk use and isn't very complicated to implement.

6. B, C. Blockchains are not currently being used to enhance password use. If anything, blockchains used to drive transaction will make things slower than existing processing tools.

7. C. The "chain" references the fact that no single hash contained in a "block" within the blockchain can be altered without affecting the others. Blockchain transactions are often intended to *not* be easily traceable to their origins. Transactions using a common blockchain technology need not be connected in any way.

8. D. The Trusted Platform Module will allow you to configure BitLocker to automatically unlock your system drive at boot time.

9. B. BitLocker is available only for Windows. eCryptfs and dm-crypt are available only for Linux.

10. B. There are perfectly justifiable reasons for not encrypting some types of data. Swap files are *not* frequent sources of malware—and even if they were, encrypting them wouldn't help. Leaving data unencrypted will *not* slow down your system.

Chapter 6: Encrypting Your Moving Data

1. A. Because it is sent from the web server to the browser on the client computer, website data is called *data in transit*. Since such data could be either static or dynamic, neither term accurately describes the general concept.

2. C. Hypertext Transfer Protocol Secure (HTTPS) is a protocol used to deliver encrypted web pages. VPNs are connectivity configurations that allow encrypted traffic across insecure networks, but they don't serve web pages. SFTP is a secure implementation of the File Transfer Protocol (FTP), which is not directly related to web content. HTTP is the insecure version of HTTPS.

3. B, D. Depending on the browser and browser version you use, a properly encrypted website will primarily be indicated by the *absence* of prominent warnings and alerts. Those browsers that display the full URL addresses will also show `https` at the start of the URL rather than just `http`.

4. C. Root certificates don't prevent page loads. Specific root certificates are issued by CAs and installed on browsers but are not used directly from CA servers. The job of a root certificate is to assure the browser that the server is encrypted, not the other way around.

5. D. The Let's Encrypt project aims to make TLS encryption certificates freely available as widely as possible.

6. C. GPG is used to encrypt files. OpenPGP is a standard defining the use of PGP encryption. HTTPS requires encryption for browser sessions.

7. A, B. Seeing how they both include the word *secure* in their names, SSH and HTTPS are both encrypted protocols, which is not true of FTP and HTTP.

8. D. SSL/TLS certificates are focused on website encryption configurations.

9. B. OpenPGP is an open-source standard for implementing the PGP standard.

10. A. OpenPGP is an open-source standard for implementing the PGP standard. TLS is an HTTP-based encryption protocol. Thunderbird is an open-source email client.

11. C. A virtual private network (VPN) is a technique for safely extending a single private network across an insecure public network. A software package that secures the remote transfer and installation of applications is a software repository.

12. D. A tunnel is an existing secure remote network connection that can be utilized by secondary processes.

13. A. Even if your source is reliable, there's no guarantee that a third party didn't alter elements in transit. Not all dangerous changes to software packages will necessarily be caught by anti-malware software. If you shut down your network connection, you won't be able to download software (or anything else).

Chapter 7: Risk Assessment

1. B. Open-source intelligence (OSINT) is data related to an organization that's collected from public archives. OSINT reconnaissance involves scanning the Internet for such data.

2. B, C. Google dorks were not created specifically for OSINT. There is, to my knowledge, no OSINT tool called FireEye. (I'll bet you were thinking about TinEye, weren't you?)

3. A. If LinkedIn admins have access to your private authentication information, you're doing something wrong. There is no such thing as "live, dynamic links" at LinkedIn. The LinkedIn site isn't built in a way that would make it easy for anyone to post significant amounts of data.

4. A. The NVD is a repository of standards-based vulnerability management data. A "source of information and tools relating to security assessments" refers to OWASP. An "organizing

structure for the collecting, categorizing, and distributing vulnerability definitions" refers to SCAP. A "naming standard for security vulnerabilities and exposures" refers to CVE.

5. D. A "declarative language that's used to contain and report a system's configuration and security state" refers to OVAL. A standard for identifying a vulnerability's target operating system and software profile refers to CPE. "Consolidating multiple OVAL result files into a single data stream" refers to ARF. A "repository of standards-based vulnerability management data" refers to NVD.

6. C. Vulnerability scanners base their ranking on the Common Vulnerability Scoring System (CVSS).

7. B. Vulnerability definitions are loaded by vulnerability scanners as part of the setup process. They are not installed by default on an OS, would not normally be downloaded from the NVD website (it's impractical), and are not available through the OWASP website.

8. B. Vulnerability definitions are delivered using the JSON format. Until late 2019, they were available in XML.

9. A, C. While Nexpose and Nessus both have lightweight versions available for free, they are not open source.

10. B. While you will use a complete set of known vulnerabilities as part of your scan, cataloging them is not the goal. Attempting to breach a network or damage data might be part of a penetration test, but not a vulnerability scan.

11. A. A network port is a numeric identifier that permits targeted routing among multiple services—like a web server using port 80 or an SSH server using port 22—using a single IP address.

12. A, B. To be as accurate an indication of the state of your infrastructure as possible, a proper penetration test should be based on as little "inside" information as possible.

13. D. A man-in-the-middle attack involves intercepting data in transit between remote locations. Cross-site scripting involves inserting malicious client-side scripts into a web page. Phishing involves tricking someone into unknowingly revealing private information.

14. B. Cross-site scripting involves inserting malicious client-side scripts into a web page. SQL injection involves injecting malicious code into a database-driven web form. Phishing involves tricking someone into unknowingly revealing private information.

15. A, C, D. While it's always helpful to have an idea of how much one attack or another might cost you, that kind of information isn't typically included in a risk assessment.

Chapter 8: Configuring System Backups and Monitoring

1. C. Ransomware attacks encrypt your system and application data, preventing you from accessing or using it.

2. A. Hardware profiles are unlikely to be useful for recovering a software failure. Similarly, there's usually no value in backing up virtual filesystems as they're generated automatically at boot time.

3. B. The RPO is a system state that's current enough to meet your organization's minimum requirements.

4. D. The RTO is the maximum length of time your organization could afford to be without an unavailable application

5. C. While storage locations can be destroyed or damaged and live application data does quickly become outdated, the question refers specifically to storage media formats.

6. A. The quality, security, and reliability of storage solutions offered by the main cloud providers are, if anything, far superior to anything most companies could achieve. Security in transit should not be a problem if you properly apply normal encryption practices.

7. B, C. Regulatory compliance practices are seldom more cost effective, and they're never a hardware requirement.

8. B. A differential backup will only copy objects that have changed or been added since the last full backup operation.

9. A. An incremental backup will only copy objects that have changed or been added since the most recent backup operation.

10. D. The nature or location of your data will not normally have any impact on this kind of decision, and the complexity of differential backups isn't noticeably greater than for incremental backups.

11. A, B, D. Backing up data incrementally is important but isn't a factor in architectural diversification.

12. A. Strong firewall projection, scalability, and well-trained engineers are all very helpful, but not specifically for preventing major physical outages.

13. D. A hot backup system maintains running and ready-to-failover copies of the latest version of your application data. Warm backups won't have the latest data already online. Cold backups need to be launched and provisioned.

14. A. JournalD and `dmesg` work for parsing system log information, but they're not active. NIDSs are active, but they don't look for filesystem anomalies.

15. A, B. Scheduling times for regular administration duties never works more than once or twice, and streaming log data in the background will guarantee that anything important will be missed.

16. C. IDSs and NIDSs will typically help only during and after an attack, and VPNs aren't in the business of data analysis. But log analysis can reveal past and current events and future-facing trends.

Chapter 9: Resource Isolation Design Patterns

1. B. Monitoring and reducing the vulnerability surface and availability of your infrastructure are important but have little to do with resource isolation.

2. A, D. Variations of Amazon's multiavailability zone setup primarily aim to provide greater availability. The primary goal of separating production environments from staging and development is to provide sandbox environments for experimenting without fear of damaging production resources. DMZs and bastion hosts exist to provide isolation to increase system security.

3. A, B. Auto scaling software and failover schemes are meant more to increase application availability rather than partition networks.

4. D. The isolation, predictability, and security promised by network sandboxes seems well described through the metaphor of a child's sandbox.

5. B, C. AWS Virtual Private Cloud (VPC) is focused primarily on network traffic, not compute environments. VMware vSphere is a private cloud virtualization platform that isn't primarily known for the speed of its deployments, but for providing a complete, robust, virtualized compute environment.

6. A, B. Forensic analysis is seldom primarily concerned with the speed of analysis or general system performance.

7. B. I'm not aware of any advantages or disadvantages between the support available for containers and for other technologies. Containers, as a rule, do not incorporate graphic interfaces. Since containers are generally meant to live for only short times, they can hardly be characterized as "durable."

8. C. The *gap* in *air gap* means that there's no connection of any sort between the isolated server and other compute resources.

9. C. Access controls in a DAC system are flexible in that they can be overridden, but only by administrator users (as in sudo users, on a Unix-based system).

10. A, C. Network ACLs and firewall routing rules are not MACs insofar as they don't operate at the operating system level.

11. C. The problem with SELinux, ACLs, and containers is that they all permit full access to an account once it's been authenticated. Since we're talking here about a compromised account, the only real protection is some kind of built-in usage limits.

Index

A

access control list (ACL), 50, 166
access point, 78
account, anonymous, 4, 6
account isolation, 144
Address Resolution Protocol (ARP), 31, 158
administrator, responsibility of, 3
ads, function of, 24
Advanced Encryption Standard (AES), 90
Advanced Package Tool (ATP), 23
advanced persistent threat (APT), 23
adware, function of, 28
air gapping, 148, 166
alert, configuring, 135–137
algorithm, 86, 90
Amazon Web Services (AWS)
  for backup, 131
  Key Management Service (KMS), 93
  limitations on, 151
  multi-availability zone setup, 166
  overview of, 52, 53
anonymous account, 4, 6
anonymous browsing session, 7
antivirus software, 53, 159. *See also* software
application firewall, 53–54. *See also* firewall
APT (advanced persistent threat), 23
archive, public, personal data on, 6–7
ARP (Address Resolution Protocol), 31, 158
assessment, risk, 114, 115–119
Asset Reporting Format (ARF), 118
asymmetric encryption, 87, 89, 94, 162

ATP (Advanced Package Tool), 23
attack. *See also* phishing attack
  brute-force, 44
  cold boot, 40
  denial-of-service (DoS), 30, 158
  dictionary, 44
  distributed denial-of-service, 30
  man-in-the-middle, 30, 121, 123, 164
  network routing, 30–31
  network-based, 30–31, 32
  proof-of-concept, 40
  ransomware, 165
  remote execution, 21
  swatting, 4, 156
attack vector, 121, 123
attribution, 19
auditing, network, 69–74, 75
authentication, 159
authenticator application, 49
authenticity, establishing, 9–11
authorization, managing, 49–50
autogenerated data, 118
automated update feature, 76
availability, of security protocol, 19
availability zone (AZ), 134
AWS (Amazon Web Services)
  for backup, 131
  Key Management Service (KMS), 93
  limitations on, 151
  multi-availability zone setup, 166
  overview of, 52, 53
  S3 (Simple Storage Service), 93, 131, 134, 138
AWS Certified Cloud Practitioner Study Guide, 31

B

backdoor, 26, 29, 157
backup
    differential, 133, 165
    example of, 128
    fast provisioning of resources for, 135
    full, 138
    importance of, 21
    incremental, 133, 138, 165
    life cycles of, 134, 138
    multitier, 134–135
    overview of, 137–138
    patterns for, 138
    on physical media, 130
    purpose of, 129–132
    ransomware and, 29
    redundancy for, 130, 138
    regulatory compliance of,
        132, 138, 165
    risks regarding, 130
    scheduling, 165
    spreading out, 131
    testing, 132
    as unusable, 138
Basic Input/Output System (BIOS),
    24, 43, 44
bastion host, 146, 147
Berners-Lee, Tim, 55
bioware vulnerability, 25. *See also*
    vulnerability
Bitcoin, 92
BitLocker, 92, 94, 162
blockchain, 86, 91–92, 94, 162
Bluetooth, 27
boot loader, 43
botnet, 21
browser, web
    attacks on, 24
    encryption and, 162
    fingerprinting, 24
    forward DNS searching by, 69
    history, personal data on, 5, 6
    password and, 46–47
    reverse DNS searching by, 69
    root certificates of, 101
    spying on, 24
    surveillance through, 41–42
    website encryption and, 100–103
browsing history, personal data on,
    5, 6
brute-force attack, 44
buffer overflow, 121
bug bounty, 114
bulkhead metaphor, 144
Burp Suite, 120

C

cache, 6
cellular network, digital espionage
    through, 27
CERT (computer emergency response
    team), 20
Certbot, 103–104
certificate, 103–104, 108
certificate authority (CA), 89, 100,
    102, 103
certificate error, 100
certificate revocation list (CRL), 103
certificate signing request (CSR), 103
cgroup (control group), 151
checksum, 107, 108
Chocolatey, 56, 160
classified data designation, 5
Classless Inter-Domain Routing (CIDR),
    66, 160
closed port, 70. *See also* network port
cloud, public, 131
cloud computing, 31, 32, 93, 131, 165
cloud firewall, 51–52
cold backup stack, 135, 138, 165.
    See also backup

cold boot attack, 40

Common Platform Enumeration (CPE), 117, 123, 164

Common Vulnerabilities and Exposures (CVE), 117, 123

Common Vulnerability Scoring System (CVSS), 118, 123, 164

computer emergency response team (CERT), 20

computer processing unit (CPU), 25, 40

computer security incident response team (CSIRT), 20

computing, function of, 40

confidential data designation, 5

confidentiality, of security protocol, 19

consumer, responsibility of, 3

container virtualization, 92, 166

control group (cgroup), 151

cookies, 24

corporation, 21, 27, 115–116

CPE (Common Platform Enumeration), 117, 123, 164

CPU (computer processing unit), 25, 40

credential, stolen, 27–28

CRL (certificate revocation list), 103

cross-site scripting (XSS), 121, 123, 164

cryptocurrency, 29

cryptocurrency miner (cryptominer), 25, 29

cryptographic hash function, 90, 94, 107

Cryptomator, 93, 94

cryptsetup, 93

CSIRT (computer security incident response team), 20

CSR (certificate signing request), 103

CVE (Common Vulnerabilities and Exposures), 117, 123

CVSS (Common Vulnerability Scoring System), 118, 123, 164

cybermobbing, 4, 11, 156

cyberstalking, 4, 11, 156

D

DAC (discretionary access control), 151, 166

dark web, 7

Darknet, 7

data

    autogenerated, 118

    breach, 27–28, 128

    classifications of, 5

    default state of, 86

    exfiltration, 22

    sharability of, 86

    in transit, 162

data, personal

    of browsing histories, 5, 6

    on the dark web, 7

    of e-commerce, 6

    exploitation of, 20–21

    on government databases, 6

    on laptop, 20

    locations for, 5–7, 11

    on mobile phones, 20

    overview of, 5

    on public archives, 6–7

    retrieving and deleting, 8

    on robot vacuum, 20

    site administrator responsibilities regarding, 7–8

    on smart home devices, 20

    on smart refrigerator, 20

    on smart TV, 20

    on social media, 6

    user considerations regarding, 8–9

data stick (USB), 24, 25–26, 42–43

Debian software repository system, 107

decryption, 87, 161

default router (gateway), 78

demilitarized zone (DMZ), 146, 152, 166

denial-of-service (DoS) attack, 30, 158

development environment, building isolated, 146–147

device
    encryption for, 89
    Internet Protocol (IP) of, 65
    Media Access Control (MAC)
        addresses of, 68
    mobile, 67
    mobile phone, 20, 56–57
    network, 78
    protecting, 41–43
    smartphone, 47, 56–57, 89, 144
    understanding, 39–43
DHCP (Dynamic Host Configuration
    Protocol), 31
dictionary attack, 44
differential backup, 133, 165. *See also*
    backup
Diffie-Hellman key exchange, 90
digital espionage, 25–27
digital privacy, protecting, 5–9
digital security, cloud computing and, 31
disaster recovery planning, 135, 138
discretionary access control (DAC),
    151, 166
distributed denial-of-service attack, 30
dm-crypt, 162
dmesg, 165
DMZ (demilitarized zone), 146, 152, 166
Docker, 148, 149, 152
Domain Name System (DNS), 68–69, 79,
    135, 160
DomainKeys Identified Mail (DKIM), 10
DoS (denial-of-service) attack, 30, 158
doxxing, 4, 11, 156
Dynamic Host Configuration Protocol
    (DHCP), 31

E

-e option, 75
e-commerce, 6
eCryptfs, 92–93, 94, 162

Electronic Frontier Foundation, 104
Elliptic Curve Discrete Logarithm Problem
    (ECDLP), 90
Elliptic Curve DSA (ECDSA), 90
email
    encryption, 104–105, 108
    phishing attack on, 10
    security of, 78
    spam filter for, 10, 12
    Transmission Control Protocol
        (TCP) and, 64
    verification, 49
encryption
    asymmetric, 87, 89, 94, 162
    blockchain and, 91–92
    certificate generating for, 103–104
    cloud computing and, 93
    defined, 90
    email, 104–105, 108
    filesystem, 89, 108
    Gmail, 105
    hashing *versus,* 90–91, 94, 162
    items for, 89, 94
    overview of, 86–89, 93–94, 108
    private key for, 87, 88
    public key for, 87–88
    purpose of, 100
    secret key for, 87
    symmetric, 87, 94
    technologies for, 92–93
    transport, 105
    usage patterns of, 89–92
    website, 99–104, 108, 156, 162
Enigmail, 105, 108
environment, development, building
    isolated, 146–147
environment, sandbox, 147–150, 152
Equifax, 27
espionage, digital, 25–27
exfiltration, 22
exploitation, of personal data,
    20–22

F

-F option, 71, 75
Facebook, 3, 6
failover, 135, 138
File Transfer Protocol (FTP), 162
filesystem, encryption for, 89, 108
firewall
    application, 53–54
    choosing, 58
    cloud, 51–52
    hardware, 51
    layers of, 159
    local (endpoint), 51–52
    network, 53–54, 58, 145–147
    overview of, 50–52
    packet, 53–54
    software, 51, 159
firmware, 43
flash drive (USB), 24, 25–26, 42–43
FlowCrypt, 105, 108
follow-up, from vulnerability scanning, 122
forensic analysis, 148, 166
forward DNS searching, 69
FTP (File Transfer Protocol), 162
full backup, 138. *See also* backup

G

gateway (default) router, 78
General Data Protection Regulation
    (GDPR), 8, 12
GitHub, 107
Gmail, 105
GNU Privacy Guard (GPG or GnuPG),
    105, 163
Google, 6, 8, 9, 105
Google Dorks, 116
government, 5, 6, 21, 26
grandmother test, 4
Greenbone, 120

H

hacker (black hat and white hat), 22
harassing cyberstalking, 4
hardware firewall, 51
hardware vulnerability, 24–25
hashing, 29, 44, 90–91, 94, 162
Have I Been Pwned? (HIBP), 28, 47–48
Health Insurance Portability and
    Accountability Act (HIPAA),
    8, 12, 132
hidden service, 7
Homebrew, 56, 160
host, 70, 72
host-based intrusion detection system
    (HIDS), 137
hosted hypervisor, 149
hot backup stack, 135, 138, 165
Hunt, Troy, 28, 47
Hypertext Markup Language (HTML), 64
Hypertext Transfer Protocol (HTTP), 52,
    53, 69, 100
Hypertext Transfer Protocol Secure (HTTPS),
    100, 159, 162, 163
hypervisor visualization, 149

I

IaaS (infrastructure-as-a-service), 31
identity theft, 22, 28, 32
IDS (intrusion detection system), 137
incremental backup, 133, 138, 165
information technology (IT), power and
    responsibilities within, 3
infrastructure, physical security of, 76–77
infrastructure-as-a-service (IaaS), 31
integrity, of security protocol, 19
Integrity Level (IL), 151
Internet Archive project, 8
Internet of Things (IoT), 20–21, 157
Internet Protocol (IP) address, 65, 78, 79, 160

Internet Security Research Group, 103
Internet service provider (ISP), 67
intrusion detection system (IDS), 137
IoT (Internet of Things), 20–21, 157
IPv4 addressing, 65–66, 68, 79, 160
IPv6 addressing, 65, 68, 79, 160
isolated development environment,
    146–147, 152
IT (information technology), power and
    responsibilities within, 3

J

JavaScript Object Notation (JSON), 118, 164
JournalD, 165
jump box, 146

K

Kali Linux, 119
Kasperksy, 29
KeePass2, 46
key, public, 87–88
Key Management Service (KMS) (AWS), 93
keylogging program, 29

L

laptop, exploitation of, 20
LastPass, 46
law enforcement, backdoor use by, 26
Let's Encrypt certificate authority, 103,
    108, 163
LinkedIn, 3, 27, 163
link-layer access, 77
Linux
    automated update feature of, 76
    booting stages of, 43
    cryptsetup for, 93
    Debian software repository system, 107

dm-crypt, 162
eCryptfs, 92–93, 94, 162
    encryption technologies for, 92–93
    hash on, 90
    Live sessions of, 42, 158
    Nmap (mapping) on, 70–71
    permissions within, 151
    Rsync, 133
    scripts on, 75
    SELinux, 151, 152, 166
    software package manager on, 56
    USB devices and, 42
    vulnerability scanning on, 119
lo (loopback), 71
local (endpoint) firewall, 51–52
local system access, controlling, 150–151
LXD, 148, 149

M

Maltego, 116
malware, 28–29, 52–54, 157
mandatory access control (MAC), 150–151,
    152, 158, 166
Mandatory Integrity Control (MIC), 151, 152
man-in-the-middle attack, 30, 121, 123, 164
Marriott/Starwood, 27
Mayo Clinic, 9
MBR defend, 159
Media Access Control (MAC) address, 68
Meltdown, 40
memory, function of, 40
Metasploit Project, 122
MFA (multifactor authentication), 10, 28,
    47, 58, 159
MIC (Mandatory Integrity Control), 151, 152
military organization, as data exploiters, 21
mitigation, 39
mobbing, 4
mobile device, network of, 67
mobile package management, 56–57

mobile phone, 20, 56–57. *See also*
    smartphone
monitoring, configuring, 135–137
multifactor authentication (MFA), 10, 28,
    47, 58, 159
multitier backup, 134–135. *See also* backup
multi-user environment, managing
    authorization within, 49–50

N

-n option, 75
NAT (Network Address Translation), 65,
    67–68, 79, 160, 161
National Institute of Standards and
    Technology (NIST), 116
National Vulnerability Database (NVD),
    116–117, 123, 163, 164
NDA (nondisclosure agreement), 5
near-field communication (NFC) protocol, 27
Nessus, 120
netmask, 66, 79, 161
network
    architecture of, 64–69
    auditing, 69–75
    behavior, securing, 77
    cellular, 27
    Domain Name System (DNS) of,
        68–69
    goals of, 64
    Internet Protocol (IP) within, 65
    IPv4 addressing and, 65–66, 68, 79, 160
    IPv6 addressing and, 65, 68, 79, 160
    items within, 64
    of mobile devices, 67
    NAT address translation and, 67–68
    Nmap (mapping), 70–72, 79
    packet analysis of, 79
    physical, 145
    ports for, 69, 79, 120, 164
    private, 145–146

public, 145–146
    scan example of, 74
    scanning, 79
    securing, 75–78
    transfer, for backup, 131
    Transmission Control Protocol (TCP)
        within, 64–65
    Wireshark and, 72–74, 79
network access, controlling, 50–55
Network Address Translation (NAT), 65,
    67–68, 79, 160, 161
network device, 78
network firewall, 53–54, 58, 145–147,
    146, 157
network intrusion detection system
    (NIDS), 137
network port, 69, 79, 120, 164
network routing attack, 30–31
network-based attack, 30–31, 32
Nexpose, 120
NFC (near-field communication)
    protocol, 27
NIST (National Institute of Standards and
    Technology), 116
Nmap (mapping), 70–72, 79, 120, 161
nondisclosure agreement (NDA), 5
nonrepudiation, of security protocol, 19
NVD (National Vulnerability Database),
    116–117, 123, 163, 164

O

object, status of, 150
one-time password (OTP), 49
onion service, 7
Online Certificate Status Protocol
    (OCSP), 103
online subnet calculator, 66
open port, 70
Open Vulnerability and Assessment Language
    (OVAL), 118, 123, 164

Open Web Application Security Project
     (OWASP), 117, 163–164
OpenPGP, 105, 163
OpenSCAP, 120
open-source intelligence (OSINT) breach, 28,
     123, 158, 163
open-source intelligence (OSINT) gathering,
     115–116, 122
OpenSSH, 64
OpenVAS, 120
OS kernel, 159
OTP (one-time password), 49
OVAL (Open Vulnerability and Assessment
     Language), 118, 123, 164
oversharing, 25
OWASP (Open Web Application Security
     Project), 117, 163–164

P

-p option, 72
PaaS (platform-as-a-service), 31
package manager, 56–57, 58
PackageManagement (OneGet), 56
packet firewall, 53–54
password
     hashing for, 29, 44, 90–91, 94, 162
     importance of, 28
     managers, 46–47
     monitoring for compromised,
          47–49, 58
     multifactor authentication (MFA), 10, 28,
          47, 58, 159
     one-time password (OTP), 49
     overview of, 43–44, 58
     policies for, 44–45
     vault, 46
     web browsers and, 46–47
patching, software, 76
path, defined, 55
Payment Card Industry Data Security
     Standards (PCI-DSS), 8, 12, 114, 132

penetration scanning, 114, 119,
     120–122, 123
perfect forward secrecy (PFS), 102
peripheral, function of, 40
permission, 49–50, 151
personal data
     of browsing histories, 5, 6
     on the dark web, 7
     of e-commerce, 6
     exploitation of, 20–21
     on government databases, 6
     on laptop, 20
     locations for, 5–7, 11
     on mobile phones, 20
     overview of, 5
     on public archives, 6–7
     retrieving and deleting, 8
     on robot vacuum, 20
     site administrator responsibilities
          regarding, 7–8
     on smart home devices, 20
     on smart refrigerator, 20
     on smart TV, 20
     on social media, 6
     user considerations regarding,
          8–9
Personal Information Removal
     Request Form, 8
personal rights, protecting, 3–4
PGP (Pretty Good Privacy) program, 105
phishing attack
     defined, 12, 156, 157, 164
     function of, 28
     overview of, 10, 121, 123
physical access, controlling, 39–43
platform-as-a-service (PaaS), 31
plausible deniability, 92
point-of-sale (POS) terminal, surveillance
     cameras near, 41
political party, as data exploiters, 21–22
power surge, 158
Pretty Good Privacy (PGP) program, 105
prevention, defined, 39

privacy, digital, protecting, 5–9
privacy settings, on social media, 5
private key, 87, 88
private network, balancing, 145–146
proof-of-concept attack, 40
protection
    of devices, 41–43
    of digital privacy, 5–9
    malware, 52–54
    of personal rights, 3–4
    of software source, 55–57
    user, 8–9
    virus, 52–54
public archive, personal data on, 6–7
public cloud, 131
public key, 87–88
public key infrastructure (PKI), 89
public network, balancing, 145–146
public vulnerability database, 116–119

R

radio-frequency identification (RFID), 26–27
rainbow table, 44, 91
random-access memory (RAM), 40
ransomware, 29, 128, 129, 158, 165
Recon-ng, 115, 116, 123
recovery point objective (RPO), 129, 138, 165
recovery time objective (RTO), 129, 138, 165
Red Hat Enterprise Linux, 151
red team/blue team exercise, 122
redundancy, for backup, 130, 138
refrigerator, exploitation of, 20
remote execution attack, 21
resource destruction, 23
resources
    Certbot, 104
    Docker, 148
    encryption of, 99–104, 108, 156, 162

Enigmail, 105
FlowCrypt, 105
GitHub, 107
Google Dorks, 116
Google's Privacy and Terms document, 9
Have I Been Pwned? (HIBP), 28, 47–48
Internet Archive project, 8
Kasperksy, 29
Let's Encrypt, 103
LXD, 148
Maltego, 116
Mayo Clinic, 9
National Institute of Standards and Technology (NIST), 116
National Vulnerability Database (NVD), 116, 118
Open Web Application Security Project (OWASP), 117
openclipart, 30
OpenSCAP, 120
Privacy and Terms document (Google), 9
Recon-ng, 116
Security Content Automation Protocol (SCAP), 116
Shodan, 21, 116
SSL Server Test, 100
TinEye, 116
Troy Hunt, 28
VirtualBox, 148
Wayback Machine, 7
Wikipedia, 102
Windows security configuration framework, 150
Wireshark, 73
ZDNet, 76
responsibility, 3
restricted data designation, 5
reverse DNS searching, 69
RFID (radio-frequency identification), 26–27
rights, personal, protecting, 3–4
risk assessment, 114, 115–119

risk management, 114
robot vacuum, exploitation of, 20
rogue host, 70
root certificate, 101, 102–103, 163
root partition, 159
rootkit, 29
router, 78
routing, rules for, 159
RPO (recovery point objective), 129, 138, 165
RSA algorithm, 90
Rsync, 133
RTO (recovery time objective), 129, 138, 165
running process, 150

S

SaaS (software-as-a-service), 31
sandbox environment, 147–150, 152
scammers, 11, 22
scanning
    bug bounty and, 114
    penetration, 114, 119, 120–122, 123
    vulnerability, 114, 118, 119–120, 122, 123, 164
SCAP (Security Content Automation Protocol), 116–117
script kiddie, 22
search history, as personal data, 5
secret key, 87
Secure Shell (SSH)
    defined, 53, 160
    function of, 99
    permission for, 52
    port for, 69, 79
Secure/Multipurpose Internet Mail Extensions (S/MIME), 105
Security Content Automation Protocol (SCAP), 116–117
security group, 52
security protocol, 19

security question, 49
Security-Enhanced Linux (SELinux), 151, 152, 166
SFTP (SSH File Transfer Protocol), 99, 162
ship building, 144
Shodan, 21, 116
shoulder surfer, 41, 158
Simple Storage Service (S3) (AWS), 93, 131, 134, 138
single sign-on (SSO) system, 49
site administrator, personal data responsibilities of, 7–8
smart home, exploitation of, 20
smart refrigerator, exploitation of, 20–21
smart TV, exploitation of, 20
smartphone, 47, 56–57, 89, 144
S/MIME (Secure/Multipurpose Internet Mail Extensions), 105
social engineering, 10, 12, 28
social media, 3–4, 5, 6, 11, 25
software
    antivirus, 53, 159
    firewall, 51, 159
    patching, 76
    repository, 56–57, 58, 106–107, 108
    source, controlling, 55–57
    vulnerability, 23–24
software-as-a-service (SaaS), 31
source, considerations regarding, 9–10
spam, 10, 12, 159
spam filter, 10
Spectre, 40
spoofing, 10, 12, 156
SQL injection, 121, 123
SSH (Secure Shell)
    defined, 53, 160
    function of, 99
    permission for, 52
    port for, 69, 79

SSH File Transfer Protocol (SFTP), 99, 162
SSL Server Test, 100, 101
SSO (single sign-on) system, 49
staging environment, 147
stalking, 4
storage, 40, 134–135, 165
Stuxnet worm, 21, 26
subnet, 66
subnet mask, 66
substitution cypher, 86
surveillance camera, 41
SWAP file, 40
swatting attack, 4, 156
switch, 78
symmetric encryption, 87, 94
system log, 136–137

T

Target, 27
TCP (Transmission Control Protocol), 64–65, 78, 79
TCP (Transmission Control Protocol) data packet, 51
TCP/IP (Transmission Control Protocol/ Internet Protocol), 30–31, 78
technology, power within, 3
Telnet, 160
threat, 10, 19–23, 32, 54–55
threat actor, 21
TinEye, 116
TLS (Transport Layer Security), 100, 102–103, 108, 163
Tomes, Tim, 115
tooling framework, 122
Tor anonymity network, 7
TPM (Trusted Platform Module), 41, 92, 162
Transmission Control Protocol (TCP), 64–65, 78, 79

Transmission Control Protocol (TCP) data packet, 51
Transmission Control Protocol/Internet Protocol (TCP/IP), 30–31, 78
transport encryption, 105
Transport Layer Security (TLS), 100, 102–103, 108, 163
trojan horse, 28
True Key, 46
trusted computing, understanding, 41
Trusted Platform Module (TPM), 41, 92, 162
TShark command (Wireshark), 75
Twitter, 3

U

Ubuntu, 92, 107
unauthorized physical access, 121
Unified Extensible Firmware Interface (UEFI), 24, 43, 44
uniform resource locator (URL), 54–55, 58
Universal Serial Bus (USB) data stick, 24, 25–26, 42–43
update feature, automated, 76
usage quota, 151, 152
user account, status of, 150
utility bill, monitoring, 29

V

vault, 93
vector, attack, 121, 123
VeraCrypt, 92, 94
verification, 159
virtual machine (VM), sandboxes for, 149
virtual private cloud (VPC), 145, 166
virtual private network (VPN)
    defined, 162, 163

overview of, 7, 108
securing actions with, 106–107
tunnel connection of, 106, 163
working with, 106–107
VirtualBox, 148, 149, 152
virtualization, container, 92, 166
virus, 52–54
VPC (virtual private cloud),
    145, 166
vulnerability
bioware, 25
data, 116–119
defined, 19, 32, 116
education regarding, 54–55
hardware, 24–25
overview of, 19–23
scans for, 114
software, 23–24
zero-day, 23
vulnerability scanning, 118, 119–120, 122,
    123, 164

W

warm backup stack, 135, 138, 165.
    See also backup
Wayback Machine, 7
web browser
attacks on, 24
encryption and, 162
fingerprinting, 24
forward DNS searching by, 69
history, personal data on, 5, 6
password and, 46–47
reverse DNS searching by, 69
root certificates of, 101
spying on, 24
surveillance through, 41–42
website encryption and, 100–103
webcam, 21

website consumer, 100
website owner, 100
websites
Certbot, 104
Docker, 148
encryption of, 99–104, 108, 156, 162
Enigmail, 105
FlowCrypt, 105
GitHub, 107
Google Dorks, 116
Google's Privacy and Terms document, 9
Have I Been Pwned? (HIBP), 28,
    47–48
Internet Archive project, 8
Kasperksy, 29
Let's Encrypt, 103
LXD, 148
Maltego, 116
Mayo Clinic, 9
National Institute of Standards and
    Technology (NIST), 116
National Vulnerability Database
    (NVD), 116, 118
Open Web Application Security
    Project (OWASP), 117
openclipart, 30
OpenSCAP, 120
Privacy and Terms document
    (Google), 9
Recon-ng, 116
Security Content Automation Protocol
    (SCAP), 116
Shodan, 21, 116
SSL Server Test, 100
TinEye, 116
Troy Hunt, 28
VirtualBox, 148
Wayback Machine, 7
Wikipedia, 102
Windows security configuration
    framework, 150

Wireshark, 73
ZDNet, 76
Wi-Fi, 26, 77
Wikipedia, 10
wireless entry point, digital espionage
    through, 26–27
Wireshark, 72–74, 75, 79
WordPress, 75
WPA2 standard, 77

X

XSS (cross-site scripting), 121, 123, 164

Y

Yahoo, 27
Yellowdog Updater, Modified (YUM),
    23, 160

Z

ZDNet, 76
Zed Attack Proxy (ZAP), 122
zero-day vulnerability, 23. *See also*
    vulnerability
zombie, 30, 158

Online Test Bank

To help you study for your LPI Security Essentials certification exam, register to gain one year of FREE access after activation to the online interactive test bank—included with your purchase of this book! All of the practice questions in this book are included in the online test bank so you can study in a timed and graded setting.

Register and Access the Online Test Bank

To register your book and get access to the online test bank, follow these steps:

1. Go to www.wiley.com/go/sybextestprep. You'll see the **"How to Register Your Book for Online Access"** instructions.
2. Click "here to register" and then select your book from the list.
3. Complete the required registration information, including answering the security verification to prove book ownership. You will be emailed a pin code.
4. Follow the directions in the email or go to www.wiley.com/go/sybextestprep.
5. Find your book on that page and click the "Register or Login" link with it. Then enter the pin code you received and click the "Activate PIN" button.
6. On the Create an Account or Login page, enter your username and password, and click Login or, if you don't have an account already, create a new account.
7. At this point, you should be in the test bank site with your new test bank listed at the top of the page. If you do not see it there, please refresh the page or log out and log back in.